ANGUS KONSTAM

san juan hill 1898

america's emergence as a world power

Praeger Illustrated Military History Series

 PRAEGER

Westport, Connecticut
London

Library of Congress Cataloging-in-Publication Data

Konstam, Angus.
    San Juan Hill 1898: America's emergence as a world power / Angus Konstam.
       p. cm. – (Praeger illustrated military history, ISSN 1547-206X)
    Originally published: Oxford: Osprey, 1998.
    Includes bibliographical references and index.
    ISBN 0-275-98456-7 (alk. paper)
    1. San Juan Hill, Battle of, Cuba, 1898. I. Title. II. Series.
    E717.1.K66   2004
    973.8'942–dc22 2004050399

British Library Cataloguing in Publication Data is available.

First published in paperback in 1998 by Osprey Publishing Limited, Elms Court,
Chapel Way, Botley, Oxford OX2 9LP. All rights reserved.

Copyright © 2004 by Osprey Publishing Limited

Library of Congress Catalog Card Number: 2004050399
ISBN: 0-275-98456-7
ISSN: 1547-206X

Praeger Publishers, 88 Post Road West, Westport, CT 06881
An imprint of Greenwood Publishing Group, Inc.
www.praeger.com

Printed in China through World Print Ltd.

The paper used in this book complies with the Permanent Paper Standard issued
by the National Information Standards Organization (Z39.48-1984).

10 9 8 7 6 5 4 3 2 1

ILLUSTRATED BY: **David Rickman**

CONTENTS

Key to military series symbols

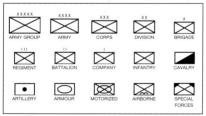

INTRODUCTION

Labelled a 'splendid little war' by Senator John Hay, the Spanish American War was a strange event in US history, caused as much by the newspapers as by political events. In 1897, support for Cuban insurgents fighting for independence from Spain was widespread in the United States, and was fuelled by the 'yellow press' in a bid to sell newspapers. When a journalist told William Randolph Hearst that there was no real war in Cuba, Hearst replied: 'You supply the story. I'll supply the war.'

In early 1898 the USS *Maine* was sent from Key West to Havana to help protect US citizens in the city. At 9:40pm on 15 February the battleship was ripped apart by a massive explosion, which cost the lives of over 250 American sailors. A court of inquiry would later blame the disaster on the explosion of a mine under the ship. The Spanish were the likely culprits.

Over the next two months both sides mobilised their armed forces and called for volunteers. The US Congress voted for a war budget, and President McKinley demanded that Spain sign an armistice with the Cubans and allow the United States to mediate. The Spanish refused. Congress then passed a resolution backing Cuban independence, and Spain broke off diplomatic relations. On 21 April the US Navy left Key West to impose a blockade of Cuba. Spain therefore declared war, and the United States officially declared war in retaliation on 25 April 1898.

What followed was one of the strangest campaigns in military history, one of a number of unusual campaigns in the Pacific and the Caribbean. The Santiago campaign was fought by two armies who both seemed to defy military logic at every turn. The organisation and supply of the American army was reminiscent of the British in the Crimean War. For their part, the Spanish commanders were more alarmed by a few hundred guerrillas in the rear than by a large modern army advancing to its front. The battle of San Juan Hill, on 1 July 1898, was fought without direction, with decisions made by privates and junior officers setting the course of the battle. The farce continued over the following weeks, when surrender talks dragged on as both parties seemed more influenced by saving face and the reaction of the press than by the military situation. 'Teddy' Roosevelt later called the campaign 'a bully affair'. 'Bully' was an apt term.

Within months of the outbreak of war, the Spanish would lose their possessions in Cuba, the Philippines, Puerto Rico, Saipan and Guam. The war marked the end of Spanish sovereignty in her 'New World', and saw the establishment of the United States as a world power.

ABOVE **Gen. William R. Shafter, commander of the V Corps, the United States expeditionary force to Cuba. Obesity and fatigue prevented him taking an active part in the battle, and he was subsequently pilloried by both fellow officers and the press. (Library of Congress)**

BELOW **Gen. Joseph 'Fighting Joe' Wheeler, commander of the Cavalry Division, US V Corps. A former Confederate general, Wheeler performed with evident skill and zeal during the campaign, despite his age and frailty. (Library of Congress)**

ORIGINS OF THE CAMPAIGN

For over four centuries before 1898, Spain had ruled over a vast and profitable overseas empire, based on her Caribbean, Central and South American possessions. Although Mexico and Peru provided the greatest source of mineral wealth (i.e. gold and silver), Cuba was regarded as the linchpin of this empire, and Havana the most important harbour in the Americas. Foreign interlopers nibbled away at the Spanish Main, and following the involvement of Spain in the Napoleonic Wars (1808–1815) many New World provinces took the opportunity to seize independence. By 1860 only Cuba and Puerto Rico were left to remind the Spanish of their former glory in the Caribbean, and Cuba was causing severe problems for the government.

Seeds of unrest had spread throughout Cuba, and in 1868, Cuban insurgents launched the Ten Year War (1868–78), the First Cuban War of Independence. Although a military failure, it provided the base from which Cuban insurgents would launch an unremitting guerrilla war against the Spanish army of occupation, destroying sugar crops, disrupting transportation and attacking isolated troop outposts.

During the Ten Year War, American sympathy for the cause of the Cuban revolution grew, fuelled by atrocity stories in the press. The end of the war brought an uneasy peace, while exiled revolutionary leaders like Maximo Gomez, Antonio Maceo and José Marti plotted to renew the struggle. By 1895 they were ready, this time with the American press following their every move. The revolution got off to a bad start, however, and the key figures of Maceo and Marti were killed.

The Spanish appointed Gen. Weyler as Governor of Cuba, and his policies were singularly effective. A *trocha* (or fortified line) was dug, splitting the island in two. A *reconcentrado* policy forced the rural population into fortified villages, but the savagery of the war and resultant destruction of crops and animals led to mass starvation. This only provided fuel for the American press. By 1897 the insurgents were crushed everywhere but Santiago, but Weyler's policies, though militarily sound, were a political disaster. He was replaced by the more lenient Gen. Blanco, but by that time the damage was done. With the American press and public at fever pitch, United States intervention seemed inevitable.

On 15 February 1898, the battleship USS

BELOW **Maj.Gen. Henry W. Lawton, commander of the 2nd Division of Shafter's V Corps. Pinned at El Caney, his command was unable to participate in the Battle of San Juan. Sketch by Frederic Remington. (Private Collection)**

Lt.Col. Theodore 'Teddy' Roosevelt, acting commander of the 1st Volunteer Cavalry Regiment (the Rough Riders). The future President of the United States secured his political future by his performance during the campaign. (Library of Congress)

Maine blew up in Havana harbour. For years, Spain's attempt to regain colonial power against a rag-tag army of Cuban insurgents had been watched by the American public, whose sentiments had been inflamed by anti-Spanish bias in the press calling for the island's independence. Public feeling had been running so high that the issue was discussed in terms of Cuban independence or war. The mysterious disaster which overtook the USS *Maine* was a spark sufficient to ignite the fire of war, and on 25 April 1898 Congress declared that a state of war had existed between the USA and Spain since 21 April. Only three days earlier, Congress had passed a mobilisation act which represented a compromise between the National Guard enthusiasts and army reformers. It called for a force made up of regulars and volunteers, many of the latter supposedly being raised from men immune to tropical diseases, such as yellow fever. Since Spain was obviously incapable of invading the United States (apart from in the overwrought imagination of a few alarmists), and since Cuba could not be freed without direct intervention, a number of regiments organised as the V Corps were sent to the ill-equipped port of Tampa, Florida, for eventual embarkation to Cuba.

Over 200,000 soldiers gathered in several camps across the United States: Chickamauga, Georgia; Falls Church, Virginia; Mobile, Alabama; San Francisco, California; and Tampa, Florida. Of these, the last became the new focus for the war effort. As the days wore on, an increasing quantity of men and matériel was gathered at Tampa, and turned into something resembling a military organisation. Few officers had experience of the logistics and planning required to perform such a task, so they had to learn everything from trial and error. The only senior officer in Tampa to have ever commanded a formation bigger than a regiment was Gen. Wheeler, who had last fought at the head of the Cavalry Corps of the Confederate army of the Tennessee in 1865. His experience was also to have a decisive impact on the outcome of the campaign.

Troops gathered in Tampa from all over America, and were formed into regiments that often had never even fought or trained together before. With only seven weeks of preparation, the volunteer troops went into battle with the bare minimum of military training and discipline. The process did at least help to turn them from jingoistic patriots into a practical army of militiamen, and enthusiasm and adaptation made up for lack of expertise during the ensuing months.

Regular troops arrived from garrisons scattered across the American West. After years of serving in small detachments and in isolated garrisons, they had rarely seen their parent regiment operating together as a unit. The learning curve of the regulars as they trained at Tampa was almost as steep as that of their volunteer compatriots. As the muddled logistical situation unravelled itself, plans were laid for sending the troops into action.

When word reached the War Department that the only Spanish naval squadron in the Atlantic was blockaded in Santiago de Cuba, orders were telegraphed to Gen. Shafter in Tampa to prepare the troops for immediate departure. Regiments scrambled for the waiting transport ships and even fought among themselves for places on board. 'Teddy' Roosevelt commandeered a ship for the Rough Riders and refused to disembark, thereby assuring a place for the volunteer cavalry regiment in the campaign. The cavalry mounts were not so lucky. Due to insufficient transports, Gen. Wheeler's cavalry were forced to leave their horses behind. Only the artillery and a handful of officers would be allowed to load their horses. Eventually, 16,300 men, 2,295 horses and mules, 34 artillery pieces, four Gatling guns and 89 journalists were loaded and ready to sail. They continued to wait for several days while the navy searched for a 'phantom' Spanish cruiser. Finally, on 12 June they were given orders to sail. The invasion of Cuba was underway.

Gen. Calixto Garçia and staff, commander of the Cuban insurgents in eastern Cuba. A gifted commander, he was criticised for not lending more support to the US army. In reality, his guerrilla tactics did much to ensure an American victory. (National Archives)

THE OPPOSING COMMANDERS

THE AMERICANS

Lt.Gen. William Rufus Shafter (1835–1906) commanded the American force in Cuba. Although not a West Point graduate, he had fought in the army during the Civil War and the Indian Wars, where he won the Medal of Honor. A former schoolteacher, he started his military career in 1861 as a volunteer in the 7th Michigan Infantry. During the Peninsular Campaign of 1862 he became a lieutenant and fought in the Army of the Potomac without distinguishing himself. He continued to serve in the army during the era of the Indian Wars in a variety of posts, participating in strike-breaking as well as in combat on the western frontier. He slowly climbed through the ranks, becoming a colonel in 1879, and a brigadier-general in 1897. At the outbreak of the war with Spain he was appointed a major-general of Volunteers, and took command of V Corps, then gathering at Tampa, Florida.

Shafter was noted for his professionalism and honesty, although he was also regarded as blunt, hard-nosed and unresponsive to political or media pressure. Described as having 'spaniel eyes', he was of average height, suffered from gout and sported a moustache. Any physical description of him, though, was dominated by his most significant feature: Shafter weighed over 300 pounds (21 stone)! His obesity was a major issue when it became apparent that he was not physically able to cope with the rigours of campaigning in the tropics. Crippled by gout and the heat, his lack of control over the progress of the campaign would

Gen. Veleriano Weyler and Gen. Blanco, with senior staff. Both were governors-general of Cuba, although Weyler, dubbed 'the Butcher' by the American press, was recalled to Spain before war was declared. Sketch by Frederic Remington. (Private Collection)

Gen. Arsenio Linares, commander of the Spanish forces in Santiago (Oriente) Province. His apparent military lethargy was due to a fear of Cuban insurgent attacks and an appalling supply situation. Sketch from *McClures Magazine*, October 1898. (Private Collection)

have serious consequences for the American cause. He retired in 1899.

Maj.Gen. Joseph 'Fighting Joe' Wheeler (1836–1906) led the Cavalry Division of Shafter's army. Short and slightly built, with a long snowy-white beard, the 61-year-old commander appeared frail. Looks were deceptive, however, as Wheeler was a tough and intelligent serving general, and possessed more military experience than any other commander, although he hadn't always fought in a blue uniform. A West Point graduate of 1859, he was made a cavalry colonel in the Confederate Army of Tennessee in 1862. Promoted to brigadier during the Stones River/Murfreesboro campaign of December 1862, by late 1863 he was a corps commander and fought in that role at Chickamauga, the Atlanta campaign and during the opposition to Sherman's march to the sea. After the war he served as the Democratic Congressman for Alabama and chaired House Committees in Washington, before President McKinley offered him a new command. Although he handed over command of the division because of illness the day before the assault on San Juan, his influence did much to ensure an American victory. In 1899 he fought in the Philippines, before retiring in 1900.

Maj.Gen. Henry W. Lawton (1843–1899) served in an Indiana regiment during the Civil War, where he was awarded the Congressional Medal of Honor and was made a brevet colonel. After the war he tried his hand at law, but quickly returned to the army: as a cavalry commander he was responsible for capturing Geronimo after a 1,200-mile chase in 1886. He commanded Shafter's Second Division, and after the Cuban campaign he was sent to the Philippines, where he was killed in action.

Maj.Gen. Jacob F. Kent (1835–1918) was another West Pointer. Born in Philadelphia in 1835, he served with distinction in the Civil War, and then spent almost 30 years on garrison duty in the South and West. He was still a colonel in 1898, but when war broke out he was made a brigadier-general of Volunteers, then given command of the First Division. Despite reported clumsiness in handling large bodies of troops, he proved a competent commander when the battle started. Criticised for showing a lack of decisiveness, he retired immediately after the war.

Col. Leonard Wood (1860–1927) commanded the Rough Riders, but on the day of the assault on San Juan Hill he took over the First Cavalry Brigade from Brig.Gen. Young, who replaced the incapacitated Wheeler as commander of the Cavalry Division. This allowed Wood's friend Theodore Roosevelt to take command of the Rough Riders for the battle. Wood was a New England doctor and Harvard graduate who joined the army in 1886 as a contract surgeon. He quickly rose to prominence after assisting in the capture of Geronimo (for which he was given the Congressional Medal of Honor). Made a captain assistant surgeon in 1889, he was recommended for the post of medical aide to

Gen. José Toral, the deputy commander of Santiago Province. When Linares was wounded, Toral was left with the task of capitulating to the Americans. Sketch from *McClures Magazine*, October 1898. (Private Collection)

the President in 1892. When war broke out in 1898, he asked to join the 1st Volunteer Cavalry, a request supported by the President. He was made colonel of the regiment, and Roosevelt became his deputy.

Lt.Col. Theodore Roosevelt (1858–1919) is perhaps the most famous participant in the campaign. A graduate of Harvard, he was elected to the New York State Assembly as a Republican at the age of 23, and became assembly speaker at 25. He also took time to write *The Naval War of 1812*, the definitive history of the conflict. He lost the New York mayoral election in 1886, but three years later he was appointed to the US Civil Service Commission by President Harrison. In 1895, he became head of the New York City Police and introduced innovative reforms. By this time his abilities were widely noted, and in 1897 President McKinley made him Assistant Secretary of the Navy. A lifelong advocate of naval power, he helped expand the fleet, and brought it to a high state of preparedness. After the USS *Maine* was destroyed in February 1898, he strongly advocated war, set the navy on a war footing and was responsible for sending Admiral Dewey to command the Asiatic Squadron. Once war was declared, he wanted to take a direct part in the conflict he had helped to start, and Secretary of War Russell Alger made him second-in-command of the 1st US Volunteer Cavalry (the Rough Riders). Although he had no military training, his impulsiveness and energy served him well when more experienced officers proceeded with caution. His ability to court the press, his talent for self-publicity and his social and political status also made him the ultimate winner of the war, but he subsequently used his fame for his own ends and denigrated the achievements of other, regular officers. Despite his criticism of the War Department, President McKinley knew a good political opportunity when he came across one, and declared Roosevelt his running-mate in the 1900 elections. When President McKinley was assassinated in 1901, Theodore Roosevelt, aged 42, became the youngest president of the United States in history.

Rear-Admiral William T. Sampson (1840–1902) commanded the US naval squadron blockading Santiago. An Annapolis graduate of 1861, he served on various Civil War ships, including the ironclad USS *Patapsco* which was sunk by a mine. He slowly rose through the ranks, even serving as head of the Physics Department of the Naval Academy. Following a three-year post as commander of a screw sloop in the Far East, a series of administrative and scientific postings followed between 1882 and 1897. In that year he was given a seagoing command in charge of the battleship USS *Iowa*. He was named chairman of the board established to investigate the sinking of the USS *Maine* during the spring of 1898, and on its dissolution, was promoted to Rear-Admiral with command of the North Atlantic Squadron based in Key West. Once the Spanish squadron was located in Santiago harbour, Sampson and Rear-Admiral Schley's Flying Squadron established a close blockade of the Spanish fleet. His absence at the start of the naval battle of Santiago resulted in a long-running controversy over who won the battle: was it Sampson, or his subordinate, Winfield Scott Schley? When considered in retrospect, it was Sampson's planning and organisation combined with Schley's leadership which brought about the naval victory.

THE SPANISH

Gen. Ramón Blanco y Erenas (1831–1906) was the Spanish governor-general of Cuba during the war. Born in San Sebastian, he served in Cuba in various military capacities including province commander and governor-general (with full military power) before returning to Spain in 1881. His successor, Valeriano Weyler, was seen as too draconian in his anti-guerrilla war, and the suffering he inflicted upon Cuban civilians hardened American opinion against Spain. When Weyler was recalled in 1897, Gen. Blanco returned to the post. On the outbreak of war he was faced with defending Cuba against both American invasion and native guerrillas. The trouble encountered by the Santiago relief column from guerrillas gives some idea of the problems he faced.

Lt.Gen. Arsenio Linares y Pombo (1848–1914) entered the army in 1860, graduating from the Artillery Academy as a lieutenant of infantry. He served in the Carlist Wars from 1867–70 fighting Basque separatists, then from 1872–4 he fought against Cuban insurgents. After a brief return to Spain, he went back to Cuba in 1875, where he was promoted to colonel after his part in the battle of Arroyo del Gato. For the next 15 years he served in a variety of administrative posts in Spain, Cuba and the Philippines, until he was given another field command in 1893, this time fighting Moroccan tribesmen. After distinguishing himself in Morocco, he was sent to Cuba in 1895, where he cleared Cuban insurgents from Pinar del Rio Province, earning himself a promotion at the same time. On the eve of the Spanish American war he was made lieutenant-general, and given command of all Spanish troops in eastern Cuba, based at Santiago.

His performance during the campaign is best described as cautious. Early on he surrendered the initiative to the Americans, and never tried to regain it. Although a brave and capable commander, he was the man responsible for the Spanish defeat. After losing an arm on San Juan Hill, he handed over command to Toral, who took the blame for the Spanish surrender. After the war, Linares continued to serve in the army, becoming Spanish Minister of War.

Brig.Gen. Joaquin Vara del Ray y Rubio (1840–1898) commanded the Spanish garrison at El Caney. He entered the army at 15, then fought in the civil wars and revolts that split Spain from 1868–76. Made a lieutenant-colonel in 1884, he then served in the Philippines fighting Moro guerrillas. Having returned to Spain to organise army recruitment in 1890, he requested service in Cuba when the fighting with the insurgents broke out in 1895. He was promoted to brigadier-general two years later for his part in the defeat and death of the Cuban leader Antonio Macías. Sent to Santiago Province, he was due to return to Spain, but volunteered to stay when war was declared in 1898. His subsequent defence of El Caney against impossible odds was the high point of the Spanish

TOP **Gen. Joachim Vara del Ray, commander of the Spanish garrison at El Caney. His desperate defence of the village against overwhelming odds gained a grudging respect for the Spanish from their adversaries. (National Archives)**

ABOVE **Rear-Admiral Pascual Cervera y Topete, commander of the Spanish Atlantic Squadron. Every inch a Spanish nobleman, he was noted for his gallantry and courage. (Monroe County Public Library)**

Rear-Admiral Winfield S. Schley, commander of the US Flying Squadron, and Admiral Sampson's deputy. As Sampson was absent when the Spanish fleet sailed, he was the 'man on the spot', and performed with flair. (US navy)

resistance to the American invasion.

Maj.Gen. José Toral Vazquez (1832–1904) came from an old military family, and joined the Military Academy at 10. He subsequently held various mainly administrative posts during Spain's civil wars and colonial insurrections of the 1840s to the 1870s, but was only promoted to brigadier-general in 1889. In 1895 he commanded the Madrid garrison, which performed security and ceremonial duties in the Spanish capital. He volunteered for service in Cuba, and that year he was sent to Guantanamo, in Santiago Province. He performed his duties well, and in 1898 he was recalled to Santiago, where Linares wanted him to serve as his deputy. After Linares was wounded, Toral assumed command of the Spanish defenders around Santiago. He was subsequently criticised for surrendering, and on returning to Spain he held no further military commands. In truth he had little option, and his performance was as good as could be expected in the difficult situation he found himself in.

Admiral Pascual Cervera y Topete (1839–1909) trained at the Spanish Naval Academy, emerging as a sub-lieutenant in 1851. He spent most of his subsequent career at sea, which was unusual in the navy of the time. He participated in the civil war fighting separatists in Murcia, and in 1863 he served as the Spanish naval attaché in Washington. From 1865 until 1875 he commanded ships operating in conflicts in South America, the Philippines and in Spain's continuing civil war. In 1887 he was made captain of the battleship *Pelayo*, the largest ship in the Spanish fleet. After this, from 1890 until 1898, he served as the naval aide to the queen, headed the Spanish delegation at the London Naval Conference of 1891, and was made Minister of Marine. In 1896, after his promotion to rear-admiral, he was the senior Spanish officer with a seagoing command. With war imminent in early 1898, he was ordered to take command of the principal ocean-going squadron present in Spanish waters. He fought bureaucracy and inertia to prepare his force for sea, and lobbied for its realistic strategic use. However, he set sail in an ill-prepared squadron, with suicidal orders from his political masters. Given this situation, he performed his task with skill and bravery, and his gallantry was noted by all who encountered him, including his American opponents. After the war he continued in service, until his death.

Tampa
US Army encampment
FLORIDA (USA)
Lake Okeechobee
14 June: Convoy sails
GULF OF MEXICO
Miami
The Everglades
ATLANTIC OCEAN
Dry Tortugas
US Naval Station & Supply Base (Key West)
Nassau
THE BAHAMAS
Key West
Florida Keys
Andros
Florida Straits
Havana MD
Light blockading by American squadrons
Matanzas MD
Havana
HAVANA PROVINCE
Matanzas
Cardenas
Sagua la Grande
PINAR del RIO PROVINCE
Bahama Channel
Pinar del Rio
Pinar del Rio MD
MATANZAS PROVINCE
SANTA CLARA PROVINCE
Morón
Cienfuegos MD
Cienfuegos
Trocha Line Puerto Príncipe MD
Isle of Pines
Júcaro
PUERTO PRÍNCIPE PROVINCE
Light blockading squadron
Puerto Príncipe
CUBA
Holguín
SANTIAGO PROVINCE
Baracoa
Bayamo
Manzanillo
Santiago MD
Guantánamo
Cape Maisi
Santiago de Cuba
10 June: US Marines land (Guantánamo)
CAYMAN ISLANDS
1 June: Naval blockade in place
HAITI
CARIBBEAN SEA
22 June: US V Corps land (Daiquiri)
Windward Passage
Port-au-Prince

Cities with coastal defences
Trocha or fortified line
0   100 miles
0   200 km
N

JAMAICA
Kingston

Cuba contained over 160,000 Spanish troops, and the Spanish governor, Gen. Blanco, was forced to defend the whole island. The greatest military concentration was in the vicinity of Havana. Cuban insurgents made communication between the provinces extremely difficult, particularly in the eastern end of the island, so each province would effectively be on its own. A *trocha*, or fortified line, divided Cuba into two, and helped prevent guerrilla movement from the east to the more pacified western side. When war was declared, the US navy sailed from Key West to enforce a blockade of Cuba, and once the Spanish fleet reached Santiago it was securely bottled up. The Americans, therefore, had control of the sea and could choose a landing site wherever they wanted. This allowed the American transport fleet to sail round Cuba en route from Tampa to Santiago without hindrance. Gen. Shafter ignored the Marine beachhead which was already established at Guantanamo, in favour of his own landing area east of Santiago.

THE OPPOSING ARMIES

THE AMERICAN ARMY

Before the Spanish American War, the American army was a small force of under 28,000 men, mainly serving in garrisons in the American West. Consisting of 25 infantry regiments and ten cavalry regiments, plus supporting artillery batteries, the army had only recently finished fighting the Indian Wars: thus many of the troops had gained combat experience. Standards of both training and recruitment were high, and the army was highly motivated. The regular army was augmented by the National Guard, a force of over 115,000 men. Although poorly equipped and of varying levels of proficiency, the guardsmen were a useful body with which to supplement the regular army in times of conflict. The National Guard's usual role was in disaster relief, policing and, more notoriously, in quelling civil unrest and strike action. A quirk of the US army was the grouping of African-American regular troops into segregated 'Negro' regiments. The 24th and 25th Infantry and the 9th and 10th Cavalry were all classified as 'Negro' units, and these 'Buffalo Soldiers' had already served with distinction in the Indian Wars. All four regiments fought in Cuba.

Following the declaration of war, the army called for 125,000 volunteers to serve for two years, and recruiting offices across the country were inundated. Many National Guard units volunteered *en bloc*, forming supplementary battalions to existing regular regiments. By August, 56,000 regulars and 272,000 volunteers and guardsmen were in uniform. These troops were organised into seven corps, most of which saw service in Cuba, the Philippines, and Puerto Rico. Of these, I, II, III and VII Corps were mostly composed of volunteers, while V Corps consisted mainly of regulars. IV and VIII Corps were mixed.

The main problem with the American army in 1898 was not in its men, but in its logistical and command abilities. Corps and division-sized formations had not been used since the Civil War, and an army administration built to deal with the supply and outfitting of 27,000 men was faced with the need to supply ten times that number. Medical facilities were poor, and only the assistance of volunteer Red Cross nurses and doctors helped alleviate the situation.

The basic organisational unit in the US army was the regiment. In theory it consisted of three battalions, each of four companies. However, following the end of the Indian Wars, regiments were reduced to ten companies each, plus two cadre companies which served as recruiting and training units. In times of war, these units would be filled by volunteers, and the regiment would fight in three battalions. In reality, the regiments sent to Cuba were sent as ten-company units, and these all fought as a single battalion. On paper, the company numbered 140

Rear-Admiral William T. Sampson, commander of the US Atlantic Squadron, and senior American naval officer in Cuban waters. He was the architect of the Cuban blockade, and he commanded the fleet off Santiago. (Library of Congress)

officers and men, but in Cuba the regiments fought at less than half-strength (averaging 520 men per regiment). Volunteer and National Guard regiments were larger, and in Cuba the volunteer regiments had an average strength of 860 men apiece. Cavalry regiments were formed into three squadrons of four companies each, with a paper strength of 100 men per company. Only two squadrons per regiment were transported to Cuba, and these fought without their horses. The average strength of a cavalry regiment in Cuba was 400 men, while the 1st Volunteer Cavalry (Rough Riders) consisted of 600 men. Artillery was organised into administrative regiments, which included coastal batteries. In Cuba the artillery fought in independent four-gun batteries, with a strength of 70 men each.

The US army fought in uniforms that were completely unsuited to warfare in the tropics. Blue flannel shirts, brown wool trousers, canvas leggings, heavy leather shoes and a felt hat constituted a uniform that invited heat exhaustion. Cotton khaki uniforms were produced, but only reached the troops after the campaign was over. Regular troops were armed with the efficient Krag-Jorgensen bolt-action rifle. It fired a .3 in. (0.40 calibre) bullet, using a five-round clip. Its accuracy was comparable to the Spanish Mauser rifle, although it was less reliable in the field. The cavalrymen carried the Model 1896 Krag carbine. Supplies of Krag rifles were limited, so the volunteer infantry regiments were issued with the Trapdoor Springfield Model 1873, an obsolete weapon that used black powder cartridges. It was considered a danger to the firer as well as the target, as the cloud of smoke it emitted when used betrayed the firer's position. The Krag and Mauser rifles of the regular troops used smokeless powder cartridges.

War correspondents in Tampa, Florida, including Stephen Crane (seated, second left) and Richard Harding Davis (standing, second left). Journalism would have a dramatic influence on the war. (National Archives)

THE SPANISH ARMY

The Spanish army had not fought a regular army since the Napoleonic Wars, but had been involved in an endless string of guerrilla wars and civil insurrections. As a result, it had become expert in counter-insurgency warfare. In both Cuba and the Philippines, the Spanish army performed well in this role, and by 1898 it was a proven and experienced anti-guerrilla force. Unfortunately, it was not prepared for a war against a conventional opponent, and the troops in Cuba lacked proper artillery support and experience in operating in large formations.

The war exposed other flaws in the army. Junior officers were often in their late teens, and products of the Spanish military academy. Others, promoted through the ranks, could be much older. The ratio of officers to men was unusually high, averaging one officer to every six enlisted men, or four times the ratio found in the American army. Immense social differences made the gulf between officer and soldier similar to that encountered in Russian armies of the same period. The soldiers, mostly in their early 20s, were for the most part poorly educated and lacking in initiative. During the war they also displayed remarkable courage and tenacity, earning praise from their opponents.

The Spanish army was organised into regiments for administrative purposes only, the battalion being the standard tactical unit. A regiment consisted of two battalions of six companies each. The paper listing of 160 officers and men per company was often under-strength in reality, particularly if serving away from its recruiting area. A full-strength battalion therefore contained around 1,000 men, although numbers varied between different types of infantry battalion. The usual practice was that one battalion in a regiment would remain in Spain and serve as the depot battalion for the other battalion on foreign service. Formations were labelled by origin or purpose: Colonial (Cuban, Puerto Rican or Philippine) or Peninsular (Spain itself) being the most common. Others, carrying the titles 'Expeditionary' or 'Rifle', were con-

Newspaper launches and naval supply vessels in the harbour of Key West, Florida, June 1898. The town would prove to be of vital strategic importance during the war, and good telegraph links ensured that reporters could file their stories quickly. (National Archives)

sidered more specialist formations, while 'Provincial' troops were local militia formations raised in the colonies. 'Volunteer' units were smaller forces raised specifically to provide local garrison troops. Battalions on active service also raised 'guerrilla' companies from volunteers, and these served as specialist counter-insurgency forces of less than 50 men apiece. A typical garrison in Cuba would contain one mounted and one foot guerrilla company. Artillery batteries of four guns each were often split into sections and scattered throughout Cuba. The 160,000 Spanish troops in Cuba at the outbreak of the war were divided into 120 infantry battalions, ten cavalry regiments, 18 artillery batteries and two engineer battalions. Most of the specialist troops including the cavalry were grouped around Havana, and took no part in the San Juan campaign.

Tactically, they placed an emphasis on fortified positions, and, at least in Cuba, these took the form of the widespread use of entrenchments, barbed wire and rifle pits. Troops would sally out from these secure positions in mobile, fast-moving columns, returning after a search-and-destroy operation or a regional sweep. A system of blockhouses was also used to provide security over a wider area, and these positions held by small garrisons provided warning of the movement of guerrilla forces in the countryside.

The Spanish infantryman was dressed in a lightweight cotton uniform of blue and white stripes and a straw hat, ideally suited to the Cuban climate. Leather boot footwear was often replaced by sandals or moccasins. Webbing consisted of small cartridge pouches mounted on a tan leather belt. A blanket was issued for bedding, and was often worn slung over the shoulder. The Spanish uniform was therefore superior to that of the American soldier, in that it was designed for use in the tropics. The Spanish soldier was also well armed. Each infantryman carried an 1893 Model Spanish Mauser rifle, a bolt-action weapon with a five-cartridge clip. It fired its 7mm rounds with great accuracy, had a knife-bayonet, and was similar to the Mauser rifles carried by the German army in both world wars.

Soldiers of the 71st New York Volunteer Infantry Regiment boarding the transport *Vigilancia* at the port of Tampa, Florida. The heavy blanket rolls were discarded before going into battle. (National Archives)

Staff officers from V Corps and newspaper correspondents on the steps of the Henry B. Plant Hotel, Tampa, Florida. The luxury hotel served as the headquarters for Gen. Shafter's Corps: journalists dubbed this period 'the Rocking Chair War'. (National Archives)

OPPOSING PLANS

The American government had prepared contingency plans for a war with Spain, and these were brought out and studied. President McKinley left much of the strategic planning to the experts and was content to give his generals and admirals as much political freedom of action as he could. In the months preceding the outbreak of war, several tentative proposals had been discussed. The American strategic plan was to establish a naval blockade of Cuba, neutralise the Spanish fleet, then transport an expeditionary force to the island. Once there, it would work in concert with the Cuban insurgents to defeat the Spanish army, capture at least one leading city, and so force the Spanish to give up the struggle.

At the same time, Admiral Dewey in the Pacific would destroy the Spanish naval squadron based at Manila, leaving the way open for an American invasion of the Philippines. A subsidiary attack on Puerto Rico would strip Spain of all her overseas possessions. The main theatre of operation would be Cuba, and it proved to be where the decisive engagement of the war was fought. In May, President McKinley approved a plan for an offensive against Havana, where 70,000 US troops would be put ashore within 12 miles of the city. Maj.Gen. Nelson Miles, in charge of the army, was doubtful of the success of an assault on Havana, the best defended area in Cuba. The appearance of Admiral Cervera's Spanish squadron at Santiago forced the American planners to rethink. The capture of both Santiago (Cuba's second largest city) and the Spanish squadron was a better prospect than a direct assault on Havana itself. Within days the orders were given to ship V Corps to Santiago.

Loaded transports preparing to leave Tampa, Florida. The troops waited for several days aboard these cramped vessels before they were allowed to sail. (National Archives)

The Spanish had 160,000 troops in Cuba, the majority grouped around Havana. The movement of troops within Cuba by road and rail was severely disrupted by Cuban insurgent attacks, so little strategic flexibility was possible, and the commander of each military province would be forced to fight on his own. In Santiago, Gen. Linares commanding Oriente Province had 35,000 men under him, 10,500 of whom were in the vicinity of the city. Harbour defences were inadequate, with many of the guns hopelessly obsolete. Press leaks informed the Spanish that Santiago would be the target of the invasion, and steps were taken to improve the defences. Linares planned to harass the Americans as they approached the city, then pin them against the line of fortifications surrounding Santiago. The annual outbreak of yellow fever was due to start within the following two months; the longer the city could hold out, the worse the plight of the invaders. Once Spanish reinforcements and supplies had fought their way through to the region, the Spanish could counterattack and force the Americans back to their boats. Yellow fever would be the Spaniards' secret weapon, as excessive casualties from combat and disease would quickly satiate the American public's appetite for war.

Shafter, on the other hand, appeared to have no concrete plan when he sailed for Santiago. Once there, he would confer with Admiral Sampson, meet with Cuban insurgent leaders and then decide how to proceed. Shafter was well aware of the threat yellow fever posed to the troops under his command. Whatever plan he adopted, the campaign would have to be resolved as quickly as possible before disease and Spanish reinforcements shifted the balance of power any further. In short, the two opposing plans are best summed up as being 'let's see what happens' and 'let's see what can happen, then make it happen quickly'.

US Marines hoisting the American flag above the earthworks of Camp McCalla, the Marine foothold in Cuba at Guantanamo Bay. The bay would serve as a secure coaling station for the US navy. (US navy)

THE CAMPAIGN

THE LANDINGS AT DAIQUIRI AND SIBONEY

The American fleet formed up outside Tampa Bay into a three-column convoy of 32 transports and five barges, escorted by a screen of torpedo boats, cruisers and the battleship *Indiana*. Progress was slow, and the fleet sailed south at a leisurely seven knots. It passed Key West, the main naval base at the end of the Florida Keys, then sailed south-east towards the northern shore of Cuba. It arrived within

US troops aboard a transport, within sight of the coast of Cuba. The fleet sailed with bands playing and lights blazing, almost as if inviting attack. (National Archives)

THE THEATRE OF OPERATIONS IN SANTIAGO PROVINCE (22 JUNE TO 30 JUNE 1898)

After consultation with naval and guerrilla commanders, Gen. Shafter decided to land his forces at Daiquiri. The outnumbered Spanish had already withdrawn to Las Guasimas. On the following day US troops marched to Siboney, which became the main American base. A probe to the north by dismounted cavalry commanded by Gen. Wheeler led to the skirmish at Las Guasimas. After a bitter fight in thick jungle, Gen. Rubin pulled his Spanish troops back to Santiago. The Americans slowly followed, establishing a forward camp at Sevilla. After a week of waiting for supplies and orders, they were finally ready to launch an attack on the Spanish at San Juan and El Caney. During this entire week, Gen. Linares refused to move out to meet the invaders, and the Spanish remained ensconced around the city. He hoped that formidable defences, reinforcements and the start of the yellow fever season would swing the balance in favour of the Spaniards.

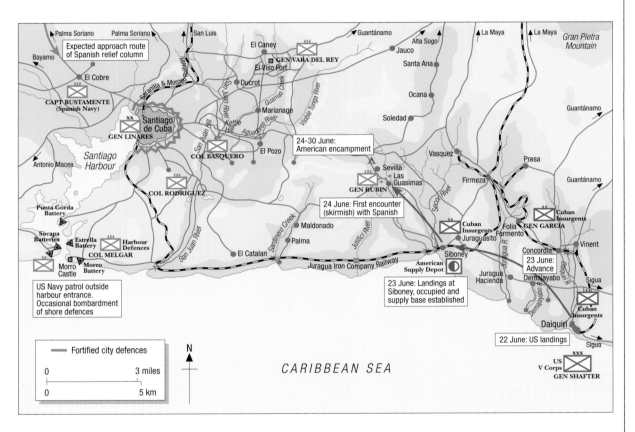

sight of the Cuban shore with lights blazing and bands playing. Foreign observers feared an onslaught by Spanish destroyers, who would find the convoy an easy target, but the attack never came. The fleet rounded the eastern tip of Cuba, then headed west, along Cuba's southern shore. It passed Guantanamo on 19 June, unaware that the US Marines had already fought a tough action to establish a beachhead. The ships ploughed on towards Santiago.

As the fleet approached Santiago on 20 June, Shafter raced ahead in a cruiser for a rendezvous with Admiral Sampson and the Cuban insurgent leader, Gen. Gomez, in the hills above the coastline to the west of Santiago. They decided that a frontal assault on Santiago's coastal defences would be extremely risky, and that the army would disembark

The Rough Riders pictured disembarking from the transport ship *Yucatan* off the Cuban coastal village of Daiquiri. This was the first amphibious landing undertaken by the army since 1865, and it was a haphazard and disorganised operation. (National Archives)

at Daiquiri, 16 miles east of the city. From there a forward base could be established at Siboney, halfway between Daiquiri and Santiago. Sampson wanted the army to clear the way for a naval attack, while Shafter saw the campaign as an army operation, with the fleet supporting his efforts. The agreement to land the troops at Daiquiri marked the highest level of co-operation that the two branches of service would achieve during the coming weeks.

On the morning of Tuesday 22 June the fleet approached Daiquiri. Five warships bombarded the shoreline around what Roosevelt described as a 'squalid little village'. The troops then began to disembark, and the operation quickly degenerated into a chaotic muddle. Some ships anchored miles out to sea as their civilian captains refused to risk their vessels. Others further inshore ran in front of the covering warships. There were insufficient launches to ferry the troops and equipment, and the high surf hindered the loading of the boats. Fortunately, Spanish resistance was minimal. The company-strength garrison retired when the bombardment started, so the Americans had the beachhead to themselves, apart from a handful of Cuban irregulars,

who came down to the beach to watch. The *Vigilancia*, carrying the Rough Riders, approached within a hundred yards of the shore, and the volunteers were amongst the first troops to land. A long jetty served as a convenient landing place, but even here the operation was chaotic. Two men drowned when they fell from their boat, and the scene was made even more bizarre by the horses, which had been cast loose to swim ashore themselves.

Col. Wood felt embarrassed that the landing was being watched by a score of foreign observers. One journalist, Edward Marshal, led a group of soldiers to an abandoned Spanish blockhouse which commanded the village. He raised an American flag on the blockhouse flagpole, and a cacophony of ship sirens, music and cheering erupted. Daiquiri was in American hands without an enemy shot being fired.

As the troops struggled ashore during that day, they encamped wherever they could around the village and for four miles down the road towards Siboney. The landing of men and supplies continued for the next two days. An advance guard led by Gen. Lawton occupied Siboney in the morning of 23 June, seven miles down the coast towards Santiago. The fleet of transports then moved itself down the coast, and Siboney became the primary American beachhead. For most of that day and night hundreds of naked American soldiers helped to unload supplies in the surf, watched by hundreds of Cuban irregulars dressed in rags. A journalist likened the scene to 'bathers in the surf at Coney Island on a hot Sunday'. By nightfall on the 23 June, only one brigade of Gen. Wheeler's Cavalry Division was ready to conduct offensive operations. With reports of a Spanish defensive position four miles to the north, on the main road from Siboney to Santiago, Wheeler was ready to exploit his advantage. Cuban insurgents had skirmished with the defenders that day, and the Spanish were reportedly digging in.

The village of Daiquiri, pictured from a transport at anchor in the bay. Surf and hidden shoals in the bay made landings difficult, and many merchant captains refused to take their ships close to the shore. (National Archives)

SPANISH SKIRMISHERS AT LAS GUASIMAS

Gen. Wheeler ordered two columns of dismounted cavalrymen to probe up the road and nearby trail from Siboney to Sevilla: the troops set off at dawn on 24 June. Cuban insurgents had already reported that Spanish troops had been seen at Las Guasimas, where the trail and road joined. Sure enough, the Rough Riders, moving up the trail in a column, were the first to run into the Spanish advanced line. A brutal skirmish developed that soon involved the larger American column moving up the main road. The Spanish defenders took full advantage of the terrain. By hiding in trees or behind impenetrable barriers of vines and undergrowth, they were concealed from the Americans. As the Rough Riders advanced, they came across a series of small clearings flanking the trail. Each of these became a miniature battlefield, where the Spanish sharpshooters occupied the treeline at the far edge and fired at the Americans as they emerged from the jungle. They then fell back to the next clearing. It was this stage of the fighting that cost the Rough Riders the majority of their casualties. The Spanish eventually fell back through Sevilla, leaving the field to the Americans.

DAVID RICKMAN

THE SKIRMISH AT LAS GUASIMAS

Before dawn on Thursday 24 June, Gen. Wheeler launched the troops of the 2nd Cavalry Brigade (dismounted) down the road towards the reported enemy positions. The rain of the night had stopped, and a wet and muddy body of troopers prepared themselves for battle. The plan was to probe the Spanish positions, with Wood leading the Rough Riders along a small trail to the west of the main road, and the remainder of the force advancing directly up the road towards the enemy. In the event of an engagement, Wood's column would be in a position to roll up any enemy opposition to the main column by attacking the Spanish in their flank.

The Rough Riders left their encampment outside Siboney at 5:40am and climbed the ridge to the north of the town. Brig.Gen. Young's column consisted of a squadron of the 1st US Cavalry (200 men), and a squadron from the 10th US ('Negro') Cavalry (220 men). Fire support was supplied by a pair of Hotchkiss mountain guns. They had already set off north along the main road from Siboney to Sevilla by the time the Rough Riders left camp. Once on the plateau above the ridge Wood located the small trail that followed the ridge on the western edge of the small valley, which ran northwards. The two American columns were therefore advancing on opposite sides of the valley, separated by just over a mile of jungle, stream and brush. Communication between the two columns was impossible due to the impenetrable terrain. The two columns would only be able to assist each other once the trails merged, at Las Guasimas. The area got its name from the

US troops landing on the coaling jetty at Daiquiri, after being ferried by naval launches. A number of soldiers drowned under the weight of their equipment as they fell from boats while disembarking. (National Archives)

Guasimas trees that grew there.

Wood was subsequently criticised for failing to provide an advance guard, but several witnesses report he sent out a five-man 'point' of Rough Riders from the Western Territories who were trained in tracking. They were led by a Sgt. Byrne and accompanied by Sgt. Fish, a charismatic and youthful New York socialite. Cuban 'guides' preceded them, and the advance guard was then followed by Capt. Capron's troop of 60 men.

The jungle precluded the use of flank guards, so the main body followed this advance guard down the trail. Col. Wood rode at the head of the main body, accompanied by Lt.Col. Roosevelt.

After an hour-and-a-half of marching (which included brief rest stops), Wood halted the column and rode forward to consult with Capron, who had signalled to his commander. At this point the trail narrowed considerably and led downhill. A barbed wire fence ran down the left (west) side of the trail, with several narrow fields of high grass beyond it. These extended back about 50 yards from the trail, and were separated by tree lines running at right angles to the trail. On the right side of the track the jungle ran beside the road, and was barely open enough to allow men to move through it. Capron reported that the enemy positions lay ahead, and he had already deployed his men in a line on either side of the road. Wood explored up the trail for a few yards, then returned with orders to deploy the column. Two troops were ordered to the left of Capron's line, and another (G Troop) to his right. Two more troops were ordered to deploy even further to the right, to attempt to link up with Gen. Young's column on the main road. The remaining four troops stayed in reserve on the trail, and a first aid station was established where the column first halted. Capron's troop then began a cautious advance down the trail to their front. It was now 8:15am.

Firing broke out first to the right of the trail where G Troop was deploying, led by Capt. Llewellyn. A correspondent following the men as they deployed reported that he 'found them breaking their way through the bushes in the direction from which the volleys came. It was like forcing the walls of a maze. If each trooper had not kept in touch with the man on either hand, he would have been lost in the thicket. At one moment the underbrush seemed swarming with troopers, and the next, except that you heard the twigs breaking and the heavy breathing of the men, or a crash as a vine pulled someone down, there was not a sign of a human anywhere'.

After a few minutes, the jungle to their front opened up into a clearing, and the Spanish fire appeared to be coming from beyond the far side, about 60 yards away. All along the American line, men returned the fire. Both sides were separated by a tangle of vines and branches, so neither force could see the enemy. Within seconds a heavy firefight ensued that spread outward from G Troop to include Capron's men and the troops to his left. To the right of the American line, two troops were still deploying. The sound of rifle fire far to the right

American troops preparing to move out from the fields around Daiquiri, heading for Siboney. The view is towards the north-west, and the village is off to the left of the camera. The hills behind Demajayabo are seen in the distance. (Library of Congress)

meant that Young's column was also engaging the Spaniards. Lt.Col. Roosevelt appeared, and ordered the troops to move to their left, cross the trail and follow Capron. This would hook the troops around the wall of vines. Because of the Spanish fire this redeployment took some time, the men having to crawl through the long grass of the clearing: eight men were left lying dead or wounded at the edge of the clearing. Roosevelt was now in command of the left flank, and was advancing to the left of the track.

By this time the columns of Wood and Young were linked by a skirmish line under the command of Capt. 'Bucky' O'Neill. Col. Wood now had a force of four troops bunched around the trail, and a further two troops linking them with Young's column on the road, about 900 yards to his right. His intention was to pin the Spaniards to their front, then outflank them with the remainder of the regiment. In reality, neither he nor any other American on the battlefield had any real idea where the Spanish positions were, or how far their line extended.

On the main track, Gen. Young's column came under fire from Spanish positions to their front and on both flanks. Fire from a number of small stone redoubts (which reportedly included machine guns) on top of a low hill prevented easy communication between the Rough Riders under Capt. O'Neill and the regulars, pinned down on the main road. Young ordered up his two mountain guns, and after a 30-minute bombardment the Spanish fire slackened.

Gen. Wheeler arrived, keen to savour his first military action since the fall of the Confederacy. He rightly assessed that his advance guard had encountered a substantial Spanish position, and ordered the rest of his division to come to their assistance from Daiquiri. The squadron of the 1st US Cavalry then pushed through the jungle to the right of the road, clearing Spanish sharpshooters from the vicinity of the two guns. The Buffalo Soldiers of the 10th Cavalry fired on the hill; then, when the 1st US Cavalry troopers joined in with supporting fire, two troops advanced in rushes, driving the Spaniards from their positions. The tide of the battle had swung in favour of Wheeler and Young. As the Americans

THE SKIRMISH AT LAS GUASIMAS (24 JUNE 1898)

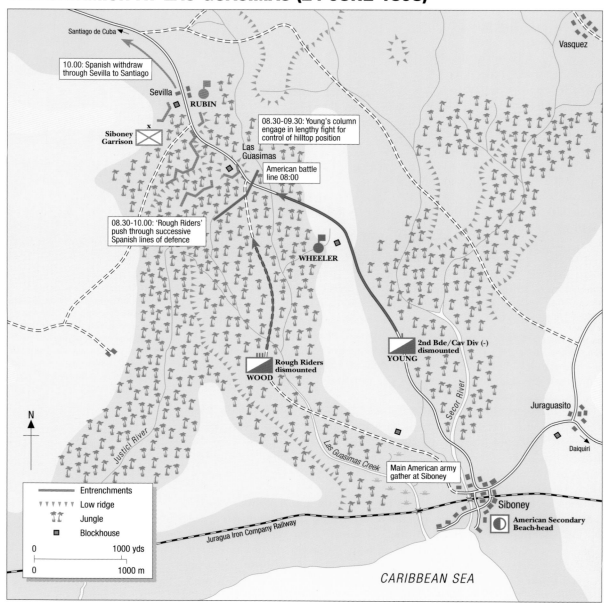

Santiago de Cuba

Vasquez

10.00: Spanish withdraw through Sevilla to Santiago

Sevilla

RUBIN

08.30-09.30: Young's column engage in lengthy fight for control of hilltop position

Siboney Garrison

Las Guasimas

American battle line 08:00

08.30-10.00: 'Rough Riders' push through successive Spanish lines of defence

WHEELER

2nd Bde/Cav Div (-) dismounted

YOUNG

Rough Riders dismounted

WOOD

Secor River

Juraguasito

Justici River

Daiquiri

Las Guasimas Creek

Main American army gather at Siboney

N

Siboney

American Secondary Beach-head

	Entrenchments
	Low ridge
	Jungle
	Blockhouse

Juragua Iron Company Railway

0   1000 yds

0   1000 m

CARIBBEAN SEA

Gen. Wheeler, a more aggressive commander than his superior, took it on himself to probe up the road between Siboney and Sevilla. Insurgents reported Spanish troops around Las Guasimas, who were a potential threat to the beachhead. While Brig. Gen. Young led a reduced brigade up the main road, the Rough Riders led by Col. Wood marched on a nearly parallel trail to the west. The two routes converged near the Spanish positions. At around 8:00am the American troops ran into the forward Spanish positions, and a confused firefight ensued. Young sent for reinforcements and used light artillery and machine guns to dislodge the Spanish from a fortified hilltop position which dominated the main road. The Rough Riders spread out to the east and west, linking up with Young's column. The American line slowly pressed forward through two successive Spanish lines. As Gen. Wheeler arrived with reinforcements, the Rough Riders took a third Spanish position in a charge. The Spanish withdrew through Sevilla to Santiago, and the disorganised Americans remained on the battlefield.

swarmed round both sides of the ridge, the Spanish were seen to fall back to a new position, 300 yards to the rear. A fresh firefight developed, but by 10:00am the Spanish withdrew out of sight.

When the former Confederate Gen. Wheeler saw the Spanish retreat, the old soldier forgot where he was for a moment, and shouted to his aides, 'We've got the damned Yankees on the run!' The American troops advanced and took the abandoned positions, but were too exhausted to pursue. As reinforcements arrived, they were pushed a half-mile ahead of the advance guard, giving Young's men a chance to recover.

Further to the west, the Rough Riders were still trying to advance. The Volunteers moved forward in a series of rushes, and each tree line became a small battleground. Within 30 minutes of the first shots the Spanish had been driven back 300 yards; but the cost was high. The score of dead or wounded included Capt. Capron and Sgt. Hamilton Fish. As Spanish fire weakened it became clear that they were falling back all along the line, and the American line followed.

Around 8:00am a second Spanish defensive line was encountered, screened by a line of vines and branches. It was at this point that Edward Marshall of the *New York Journal* was hit, one of two civilians who received a commendation in the official despatches after the battle. The Spaniards fell back after a brief exchange of shots, and as the jungle opened up into increasingly large areas of tall grass, the Americans found the ground began to slope uphill. Ahead lay a large clearing, and at its far edge lay a tree line and a ruined distillery building, 200 yards

Naval launches landing troops and supplies on the new beachhead at Siboney. Despite a constant surf, this was chosen as the principal American supply base. (National Archives)

from the American line. A flurry of shots showed that the tree line formed part of a major Spanish position. The distillery building became the focal point of the attack.

Until this point the terrain had forced the Rough Riders to break into small groups. On the edge of the field Wood and Roosevelt organised their regiment, with the two senior officers stationed at either end of a line. It is unclear whether Wood or Roosevelt ordered the regiment to advance, or whether it resulted from a spontaneous movement by the rank and file. A reporter commented that Wood was calm under fire, but that Roosevelt 'jumped up and down' with eagerness. The advance was subsequently christened 'Wood's Bluff', as the Spaniards thought the Rough Riders were the skirmish line of a much larger force. The line ran into the field, cheering as it advanced. The Spanish opened up on the attackers with a succession of disorganised volleys, causing several casualties. Their fire was insufficient to halt the attack, and as they approached the Spanish position the American cheer grew to the pitch where it was subsequently compared to the 'Rebel yell' of the Civil War. The Spaniards broke and ran back through the trees in confusion. The Rough Riders lay around the building awaiting orders.

One Spanish witness said: 'When we fired a volley, instead of falling back they came forward. This is not the way to fight.' Another Spaniard reported to his officers that 'they tried to catch us with their hands'. The Rough Riders had come through their baptism of fire relatively unscathed. Of the 534 men in the unit, eight were killed and 34 wounded. Young's column of 464 men had eight men killed and 18 wounded. The Spanish made light of the skirmish, and on 25 June the

Spanish soldiers at Santiago de Cuba. The Americans were contemptuous of their opponents until they met them in combat. The Spanish performance at El Caney demonstrated the skills of the individual Spanish soldier. (National Archives)

ABOVE **Cuban insurgents watching the Americans set up camp at Siboney. The guerrillas made a poor impression on the Americans, and observers complained of their lack of military enthusiasm.** (National Archives)

LEFT **Buffalo Soldiers of the US 10th 'Negro' Cavalry Regiment, photographed on San Juan Heights. Although misguidedly criticised by Roosevelt, other observers described them as 'some of the bravest men I know'.** (National Archives)

THE AMERICAN ADVANCE
UP THE CAMINO REAL

The American troops earmarked for
the assault on San Juan Heights rose
soon after dawn on 1 July 1898. They
had spent the night in bivouacs strung
out along the road between El Pozo and
Sevilla. As the Camino Real narrowed, the
initial four-deep column was reduced to a
line only two abreast. As the lead troops
passed through El Pozo settlement, the
nearby artillery battery fired, bringing down
counter-battery fire. Shells fell beside the
column, killing a number of soldiers. As the troops
continued down the road they came under Spanish
rifle fire, both from the troops on the Heights and
from sharpshooters hidden in the woods. Since the Spanish
Mauser rifle used a smokeless cartridge, the attackers remained hidden.
An observation balloon accompanied the troops, tethered to a wagon
that moved down the road with them. This did little but serve as a
range marker for Spanish fire, and casualties mounted as the
Spanish shells and bullets found their mark. Some of the
heaviest American casualties of the battle were inflicted during
the final stages of the approach march, and at the place
where the road crossed the San Juan River. The shallow
crossing was later dubbed the 'Bloody Ford'.

Espagna, a Santiago newspaper, even reported that 'the column of Gen. Rubin … was attacked yesterday afternoon. This morning large forces of the enemy with artillery attacked said column anew. Their attack was made with vigour, and they fought without being under cover. They were repulsed with heavy losses'. Another Spanish report claimed that 4,000 Spaniards were attacked by 10,000 Americans, and the attackers suffered 265 casualties. In reality, the first battle of the war was nothing more than a confused and bloody skirmish. 1,500 Spaniards had been attacked by 1,000 Americans and been driven from their positions. The main American force was still disentangling itself from its beachheads, and its commander was completely unaware that a battle was being fought.

The Spanish commander was reluctant to deploy his men too far in advance of his fortified positions around Santiago. Linares was still not convinced that the American landing was more than a diversion. Pulling his best troops away from Santiago would leave the city open to a second American landing or worse, a major attack by Cuban insurgents. Rubin achieved his limited objective of delaying the American advance, then withdrew back to the main perimeter around Santiago. Wheeler achieved his aim of clearing the way for the main army to advance on Santiago. Gen. Lawton, the designated leader of the V Corps advance, was furious with Wheeler for stealing the glory, but the old war-horse supplied the American public with the first victory of the war. The press considered that the American troops had been led into an ambush, but acclaimed the actions of the Rough Riders and Roosevelt. It was almost as if the regulars and Wood were merely supporting actors in a melodrama. This slant on press reporting was to continue throughout the campaign.

Gen. Shafter read the Spanish version of the skirmish, then quipped that: 'reports from Spanish sources from Santiago say we were beaten, but persisted in fighting, and they were obliged to fall back!' It was in fact a fairly accurate version of events at Las Guasimas.

PRELUDE TO BATTLE

During the afternoon of 26 June the Americans tried to take stock of their situation. Cuban irregulars, sent after the retreating Spanish, reported that there were now no Spanish troops between the American army and San Juan Heights, a mile outside the city of Santiago. Shafter ordered that Wheeler was to conduct no more 'probes', but was to entrench and hold the positions. Clearly he was unwilling to risk committing his army until all his troops were ashore and capable of supporting each other. The commanders on the field, Lawton and Wheeler, decided to interpret Shafter's orders rather more loosely. Two miles ahead lay the village of Sevilla, where the road was flanked by the Aguadores River. This offered a better defensive position, and would be closer to Santiago when the time came to attack the Spanish again. That afternoon the Americans continued their advance to Sevilla and encamped around the village. Shafter had little option but to make this his base. For the next six days the army slowly gathered around Sevilla and hauled up supplies and guns along the grandly named Camino Real (Royal Road), described by some as being no better than 'a mud slide'.

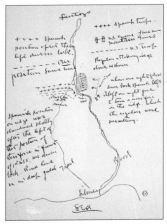

TOP **Las Guasimas, the site of the first engagement between Spanish and American troops. This was the position on the track occupied by the head of the Rough Riders column when it ran into the leading Spanish outposts. (National Archives)**

ABOVE **Sketch by Col. Leonard Wood, commander of the Rough Riders. The crosses show the forward Spanish positions at Las Guasimas, the hill taken by Gen. Wheeler and the battle line of the Rough Riders. (Monroe County Public Library)**

Engineers worked on improving the road, laying 'corduroy road' sections of logs to try to keep the wagons out of the mire. As sentries guarded the positions and learned to tell the difference between nocturnal Spanish raiders and land crabs, the remaining soldiers rested in their bivouacs. On 27 June Gen. Shafter came ashore and set up his headquarters in the village.

Gen. Wheeler complained to Shafter that the positions around Sevilla were becoming too crowded, and asked for permission to advance a few miles up the road to El Pozo ('the Fountain'), a low hill which was named after the hacienda lying at its eastern foot. After being issued strict instructions not to bring on another action, Wheeler advanced one and a half miles west to El Pozo, where he found himself overlooking the Spanish positions on San Juan Hill. To his left was the sea, hidden behind a hill. To his right were the foothills of the Sierra Maestra Mountains, and the village of El Caney. Ahead of him the Camino Real crossed the San Juan River: behind the river lay the San Juan Heights. One and a half miles from El Pozo hill, a Spanish blockhouse crowned the 150-foot-high ridge of the Heights. Slightly in front and to the right of this ridge was the smaller Kettle Hill, topped by a sugar refining 'kettle'. Through a dip in the Heights the observers saw the outskirts of the city of Santiago. Spanish soldiers were visible on San Juan Heights and Kettle Hill, preparing a fortified line of trenches and barbed wire. Any attack would have to be launched soon, before these defences became impregnable. Cuban irregulars reported that an additional 500 Spaniards were fortifying the village of El Caney, to the north, which could pose a threat to any American advance on San Juan Heights as it lay on the American's flank. Any move to outflank San Juan Heights would be impossible until El Caney had been captured. Other Cuban reports indicated that a relief force of several thousand men was approaching Santiago from the west. The attack had to be launched before these fresh troops arrived. Once the Americans held the Heights they could dig in and bombard the city until it surrendered.

The war correspondent Richard Harding Davis noted the activities of the Spanish: 'A long yellow pit opened up in the hillside of San Juan, and in it we could see straw sombreros rising and bobbing up and down, and under the shade of the blockhouse, blue-coated Spaniards strolling leisurely about ...' In his report Davis went on to criticise Shafter for his inaction.

In the opinion of most Americans in the expeditionary force, time was on the side of the Spanish. Any delay would allow them to complete their fortifications, and to call in fresh troops from the surrounding countryside. Yellow fever and other tropical diseases would only further deplete American numbers and morale. The Americans were unaware, however, that the Spanish had their own problems.

When Shafter reached El Pozo he assessed the situation and realised that he would have to neutralise El Caney. Access to the north meant that he could improve links with the Cuban irregulars and possibly even cut off the city water supply, which ran by pipe south from the Sierra Maestra Mountains. One division would take no more than a couple of hours to clear El Caney. During that time the rest of the army would advance and deploy for an attack on San Juan Heights. The El Caney division could then attack the Heights from the north-east just as the main army launched a frontal attack on the Spanish defences. The defences could be rolled up from north to south before nightfall.

Gen. Shafter returned to Sevilla and began drawing up orders for the attack, which would be launched the following day, Sunday 1 July 1898. Gen. Lawton's 2nd Division was to march off to the north immediately, and bivouac overnight just short of El Caney. The following morning Lawton would attack the village using all three of his brigades and a supporting artillery battery. The First Division and the Cavalry Division would move forward to El Pozo and wait for orders to attack the Heights the next day. A second artillery battery was ordered to deploy on El Pozo hill, where it could fire on the Spanish positions. At around 4:00pm, Lawton's men began moving out of Sevilla. Battle was about to be joined, the first major action fought by an American army since April 1865.

Bodies of two dead Rough Riders lie in a clearing, while senior officers hold an impromptu conference behind them. The regiment lost eight men at Las Guasimas. (Franklin D. Roosevelt Library)

THE BATTLES OF 1 JULY

THE SPANISH DEFENCES

The Spanish had not just waited passively to be attacked since the skirmish at Las Guasimas. Over two miles of trenchworks snaked back and forth along the San Juan Heights, part of a hastily prepared fortified line that extended from Aguadores on the coast to El Caney, eight miles to the north-east. The forward positions of this line were for the most part sited on high ground to the east of the San Juan River. The principal area of defence was itself on San Juan Heights, and an impressive line of trenches defended the area around the San Juan blockhouse. The flanking sections of the Heights were also lined with trenches forming almost a second line, where Spanish troops could protect the flanks of the main position. Barbed wire and gun pits completed the obstacles facing the Americans on the Heights, but both guns and wire were in such short supply that the wire was placed in areas where the guns had no clear line of fire. Earth from the trenches was removed to the rear slope of the Heights, to partially hide the earthworks. A forward position on Kettle Hill allowed the Spanish infantry to command the tree line less than 500 yards away, where the Camino Real road and another trail emerged from the jungle. This was

BELOW **Officers and war correspondents conferring after the skirmish at Las Guasimas. This is the same impromptu conference seen in the preceding photo. Wheeler is second from the left, and Roosevelt and Woods can be seen conferring in the background. (National Archives)**

the expected American axis of advance. The barbed wire was mainly stretched in front of Kettle Hill, on both banks of the San Juan River. The Americans were therefore facing what amounted to three lines of defence. The inner defences of the city of Santiago provided a fourth line. Centred on the Fort Canovar and the Reina Mercedes Barracks, Spanish reinforcements were held in reserve, 500 yards behind the front line.

Two miles north of the San Juan blockhouse the Spanish defensive line stopped at a point where it overlooked the stone bridge crossing the San Juan River. The bridge carried the road from Santiago to El Caney, and was by far the best metalled road on the battlefield. This provided another avenue for reinforcements to reach the fortified village. El Caney itself was sited two miles north-east of the stone bridge, and almost four miles from the American forward positions at El Pozo. A tiny track passed the hamlet of Marianage along the way. El Caney itself was a small village of palm-thatched huts and tin-roofed buildings, but did boast a large stone church.

The village had only one previous claim to fame: Cortez was supposed to have prayed in the church the night before he sailed off to conquer Mexico. The village that witnessed the beginnings of the Spanish Empire would also play a part in its demise. Strategically, El Caney guarded the flank of the Spanish position, and also posed a threat to any American advance on San Juan. Spanish reinforcements could use it as a secure point to launch a counterattack against the exposed American left flank.

The principal defensive position within the village perimeter was a substantial stone fort called El Viso, larger than the normal Spanish

Artillery supplies and ammunition being brought up by pack animals along the Camino Real between Las Guasimas and Sevilla. In places the misleadingly named 'Royal Road' was little more than a dirt track. (National Archives)

blockhouse. Sited on a hillock 400 yards south-east of the village, it commanded the approaches to the Spanish position from the south and east. Four blockhouses protected the village itself, and the village perimeter and El Viso Fort were ringed by a line of trenches, rifle pits and barbed wire. Inside the village, buildings were loop-holed and prepared as a final defensive line.

Other approaches to Santiago were also defended. The Spanish still feared another American landing, either to the west of the city or at the harbour entrance itself. Consequently, many Spanish troops were deployed to defend Morro Castle, which dominated the harbour entrance, as well as the secondary coastal batteries flanking both sides of the harbour channel. Fear of Cuban insurgent attacks also tied down troops in defences to the west of the city, around the village of El Cobre. The inner ring of city defences bristled with guns, wire and well-constructed forts, blockhouses and trenches. A direct assault on the city or on its harbour defences would be a costly undertaking. A further line of small blockhouses lined the hills to the north, guarding the city water supply from guerrilla attacks.

Despite the substantial defensive positions built by the Spanish, their defences were flawed by a simple lack of troops. Most of those that were in the area were not in a position to defend against a direct American assault. On 22 June, Gen. Linares called for 3,600 reinforcements from the town of Manzillo, 45 miles to the west. 1,000 sailors from the fleet guarded the western approaches to the city, while a further 1,200 guarded the coastal defences. A garrison of 500 men was stationed at

Building a corduroy road over the worst stretches of muddy stream crossings on the road from Las Guasimas to Sevilla. Poor conditions made supplying the army an almost impossible task. (National Archives)

El Caney, and a further 500 manned the entrenchments on San Juan Heights and Kettle Hill. This left over 9,000 more soldiers, engineers, gunners, volunteers and civil guards in the city itself and its inner defensive perimeter. Why didn't Linares bolster his front line on San Juan Heights, the obvious area for the Americans to attack?

Even before the Americans landed at Daiquiri, the Spanish troops in Santiago Province were in dire straits. Supplies were low, and guerrilla action meant that local contractors were unable to easily replenish their stocks of meat and grain from the surrounding countryside. Similarly, poor administration in the Army High Command meant that military supplies were not reaching the province. Gen. Garçia and his Cuban guerrillas had effectively isolated the city. The naval blockade by the US navy meant that resupply by sea was out of the question, and guerrilla attacks also prevented the supply of isolated posts some distance from the city. By the time the Americans landed, the garrison and inhabitants of Santiago had only enough food for a month. Although over 12,000 troops were scattered elsewhere in the province, there were not enough supplies in the city to feed the extra mouths. The troops would have to remain dispersed until supplies could reach the city. Similarly, the numbers of Cuban insurgents massing in the hills around the city was estimated at around 15,000. Gen. Linares' main fear was that guerrillas would attack Santiago and destroy his few remaining supplies while his forces were pinned by the Americans and unable to respond. The Spanish general therefore kept his troops in readiness within the city and awaited developments.

The call for reinforcements from Manzillo also included a plea for food and ammunition. Once these supplies arrived, the Spanish might be able to concentrate their forces and bolster their defences. After the skirmish at Las Guasimas, it was felt that an offensive action was unnecessary. By creating an impregnable defensive position, and with the yellow fever season approaching, the Spanish hoped that the American army would simply wither away.

Troopers of the Cavalry Division fording the Aguadores River near El Pozo, on their way up the Camino Real, shortly after dawn on 1st July 1898. The Spanish were only one and a half miles away, and soon the column would come under heavy fire. (National Archives)

SHAFTER'S PLAN

During the late afternoon of Saturday 30 June, columns of US troops snaked their way up the trail from Sevilla to El Pozo. 'Regiment after regiment passed by' noted Roosevelt, 'varied by bands of tatterdemalion Cuban insurgents, and by mule trains with ammunition.' The army bivouacked around El Pozo by midnight, and waited for dawn.

Gen. Shafter and his aides had already seen the Spanish trenches on the San Juan Heights, and the plan to capture them was brutally simple. Lawton's division would capture El Caney, thus securing the army's right flank. It would then move south-west to attack San Juan Heights. It was estimated that the El Caney operation would last two hours. The two remaining divisions of the army would march down the road from El Pozo to Santiago, which ran alongside the Aguadores River. The trail emerged from the jungle into an open grassy plain which formed the meadowland surrounding the shallow San Juan River. Beyond this lay the Heights, and the Spanish. The army would simply enter the meadow, deploy, cross the San Juan River, make a frontal assault on the Heights, and thus win the day. Once the Heights were in American hands, the city of Santiago and the fleet in its harbour would lie at the mercy of the invaders. Shafter wrote: 'It was simply going straight for them. If we attempted to flank them or dig them out … my men would have been sick before it could be accomplished, and the losses would have been many times greater than they were.' A newly-arrived Michigan volunteer regiment would make a diversion along the coast from Siboney towards Aguadores in an attempt to prevent troops reinforcing the Heights. Apart from the El Caney operation, there was no other subtlety to the plan. Inter-service rivalry also made Shafter decline the navy's offer of gunfire support, and the same reason prompted him to keep veteran US Marine reinforcements out of the fight. This was going to be the army's big day.

Gen. Wheeler was laid low with fever, and Gen. Sumner assumed

A US column marching forward past Sevilla towards El Pozo during the early evening of 30 June 1898. Gen. Shafter's headquarters were immediately behind the photo, on the northern outskirts of Sevilla. (National Archives)

command of the Cavalry Division. Young was also sick, and his place as brigade commander was taken by Col. Wood, leaving Lt.Col. 'Teddy' Roosevelt to assume command of the Rough Riders. As the senior officers prepared their troops that night, they and the ever-present journalists noted an air of intense excitement. After months of waiting, the next day would bring about the deciding battle of the war. Lt.Col. McClernand, Gen. Shafter's adjutant general, found that his commander would not be directing the battle. 'At 3:00am on the morning of July 1 I entered the tent of the Commanding General. He said he was very ill as a result of his exertions in the terrifically hot sun of the previous day, and feared he would not be able to participate as actively in the coming battle as he had intended.' It fell upon the divisional commanders (Kent and Sumner) to direct operations. In practice, they would mostly be unable to directly influence the battle due to geographical factors, and effective control devolved to brigade and regimental commanders. As Roosevelt put it, 'the battle simply fought itself'.

At the same time on the Spanish side of the lines, Gen. Arsenio Linares was also awake in his headquarters at Fort Canosa, between the Heights and the city. With only 10,000 troops available, his lines were spread thinly. Starvation already threatened the city, and troops had to be deployed to protect the roads to the west, guard outlying villages with their food supplies and secure the aqueduct supplying the city. The

An overturned supply wagon at a ford crossing outside Sevilla. Inadequate provision of supplies would delay the advance of the army beyond Sevilla for almost a week. (National Archives)

threat from Cuban insurgents meant that only 521 men waited for the Americans on San Juan Heights supported by two Krupp light artillery pieces. A further 1,000 men waited at Fort Canosa in case they were called upon to reinforce the Heights.

THE BATTLE FOR EL CANEY

The 6,650 men of Gen. Lawton's US Second Division approached El Caney at dawn on 1 July 1898. They had marched north up the track from El Pozo, passing through the hamlet of Marianage on the way. Two sections, comprising two light 3.2 in. field guns each, supported the troops. The artillery was under the command of Capt. Allyn Capron, whose son had been killed at Las Guasimas. They deployed into position on a low hill covered in bushes, about a mile to the south of El Viso fort, which was regarded as the linchpin of the Spanish defences, and would be the principal target. Meanwhile, the infantry moved forward, Gen. Ludlow's brigade circling to the left of the village and Gen. Chaffee's to the right, towards the high ground to the east of the fort. The brigade commanded by Evan Miles was still marching up from Marianage. The time was now 6:35am, and Capron was given permission to open fire.

The Spanish inflicted so many casualties on the 22nd Massachusetts Volunteers that the regiment was pulled back into reserve. Smoke from their obsolete black-powder weapons had betrayed their positions to the Spanish, who could return the fire with greater accuracy. The struggle carried on for most of the day. Once the fort of El Viso had been captured by an American assault, the Spanish pulled back to a last line of defence in the village itself, and were only finally overcome after bitter fighting. Although hopelessly outnumbered, they had held up Lawton's division long enough to prevent them from participating in the main battle for San Juan Heights.

DAVID RICKMAN

Their guns were considered obsolete by contemporary military standards. Not only did they fire black-powder shells that created tell-tale smoke, giving away the battery position, but they were not self-recoiling, which hindered accuracy as well as speed of reloading: nor were they fitted with sights to allow indirect fire. As an American artillery officer put it: 'Yet such was our backwardness in military science that the whole army was ignorant of the tremendous advance in Field Artillery that in 1898 was an accomplished fact.'

Capt. Lee, a British military observer from the Royal Engineers, recalled the scene before the battery opened fire: 'Profound quiet reigned, and there was no sign of life beyond a few thin wisps of smoke that curled from the cottage chimneys. Beyond lay a fertile valley, with a few cattle grazing, and around us on three sides arose, tier upon tier, the beautiful Sierra Maestra Mountains, wearing delicate pearly tints in the first rays of the rising sun.' This peace was about to be shattered.

Although the guns were trained on the fort, the first target to present itself was a group of horsemen, riding towards the American position from the village. The barrage overshot the target, which was fortunate, as the riders later turned out to be Cuban allies, 50 insurgents who had been keeping the village under observation. The horsemen disappeared from sight and the guns began firing on the fort. Rifle fire from the village perimeter opened up in response. While the Spanish used smokeless powder for their Mauser cartridges, the American artillerymen revealed their position with the smoke from their guns. However, despite the obsolescence of the artillery the shells were beginning to make an impression. One of the shots breached the stone wall of the fort, and a barrage lasting just over three hours caused visible damage to the fort and its surrounding earthworks, but failed to stop the hail of fire coming from the Spanish trenches. Capt. Lee reported seeing the Spanish soldiers in their 'light blue pyjama uniforms and white straw slouch hats' dive for cover into their slit trenches. 'A fresh row of hats sprouted from the ground like mushrooms and marked the position of the deep rifle pits and trenches on the

Capt. Allyn Capron with his battery officer at dawn on 1 July. The battery is shown in the position it established during the night, and is waiting for orders to open fire on the Spanish fort of El Viso. No Spanish guns were in a position to return the fire. (National Archives)

The village of El Caney, viewed from the ridge containing El Viso Fort. The church is on the right of the picture, where the final Spanish resistance was overcome. (National Archives)

glacis of the fort and at various points around the village. For the next quarter of an hour our battery kept up a leisurely fire upon the stone fort, eliciting no reply, and so little disturbing the white hats that someone suggested they were dummies.'

By this time, Gen. Chaffee's brigade had worked its way round to the hills to the east of the village, and brought down a continuous return fire on the defenders. Their position also served to cut off any chance of Spanish retreat north into the hills, and a small number of Cuban irregulars supported the extreme right flank of Chaffee's position. Meanwhile, Gen. Ludlow's brigade took up positions south of the village, supporting the battery with rifle fire. Ludlow extended his left flank as far as the Santiago to El Caney road, so he was in a position to intercept any relief attempt from the city. A sunken section of trail to the east of the village provided an improvised form of trench, and served to anchor the left flank of the American line. At this point it was within 100 yards of the western edge of the village, and under constant rifle fire from the fortified houses. Col. Miles was still approaching the battlefield with the 3rd Brigade of Lawton's division, and the head of his column passed Capron's battery at 11:00am. Miles was ordered to hold the centre, facing the El Viso Fort, and when ordered, his troops were to advance on the fort in support of Chaffee's brigade. A fourth, Gen. Bates' independent brigade, was still moving up to join Lawton's forces from El Pozo and Marianage. Although the four American guns helped to reduce the fort, the battle was to be decided by rifle fire.

49

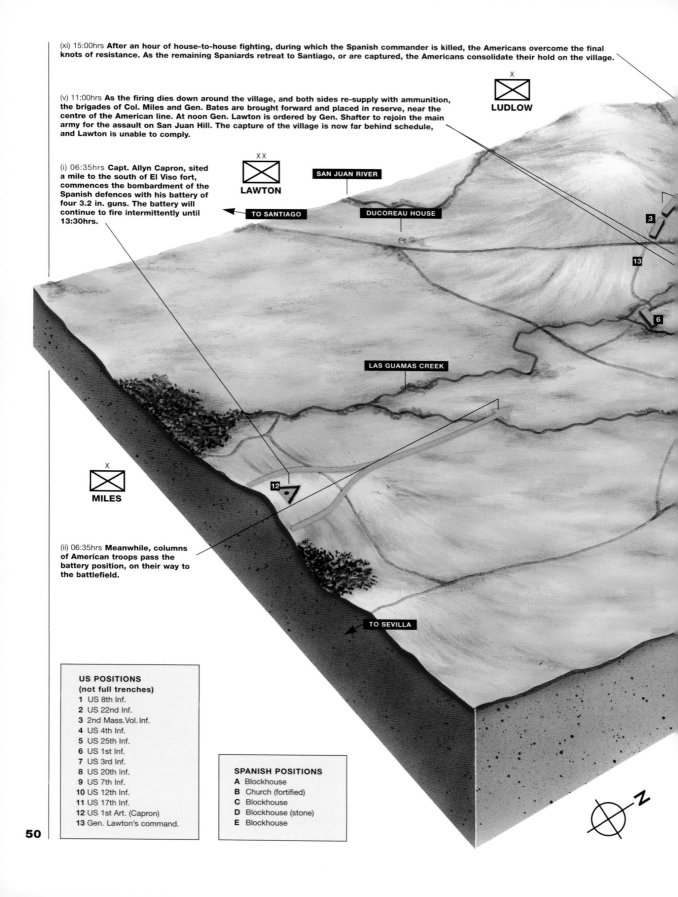

(xi) 15:00hrs **After an hour of house-to-house fighting, during which the Spanish commander is killed, the Americans overcome the final knots of resistance. As the remaining Spaniards retreat to Santiago, or are captured, the Americans consolidate their hold on the village.**

LUDLOW

(v) 11:00hrs **As the firing dies down around the village, and both sides re-supply with ammunition, the brigades of Col. Miles and Gen. Bates are brought forward and placed in reserve, near the centre of the American line. At noon Gen. Lawton is ordered by Gen. Shafter to rejoin the main army for the assault on San Juan Hill. The capture of the village is now far behind schedule, and Lawton is unable to comply.**

LAWTON

SAN JUAN RIVER

(i) 06:35hrs **Capt. Allyn Capron, sited a mile to the south of El Viso fort, commences the bombardment of the Spanish defences with his battery of four 3.2 in. guns. The battery will continue to fire intermittently until 13:30hrs.**

TO SANTIAGO

DUCOREAU HOUSE

3

13

6

LAS GUAMAS CREEK

12

MILES

(ii) 06:35hrs **Meanwhile, columns of American troops pass the battery position, on their way to the battlefield.**

TO SEVILLA

US POSITIONS
(not full trenches)
1 US 8th Inf.
2 US 22nd Inf.
3 2nd Mass.Vol. Inf.
4 US 4th Inf.
5 US 25th Inf.
6 US 1st Inf.
7 US 3rd Inf.
8 US 20th Inf.
9 US 7th Inf.
10 US 12th Inf.
11 US 17th Inf.
12 US 1st Art. (Capron)
13 Gen. Lawton's command.

SPANISH POSITIONS
A Blockhouse
B Church (fortified)
C Blockhouse
D Blockhouse (stone)
E Blockhouse

N

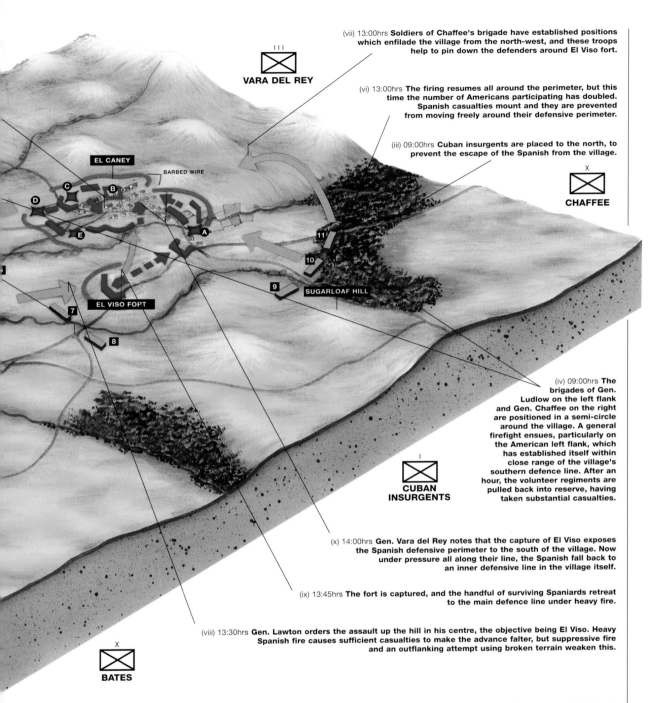

VARA DEL REY

(vii) 13:00hrs **Soldiers of Chaffee's brigade have established positions which enfilade the village from the north-west, and these troops help to pin down the defenders around El Viso fort.**

(vi) 13:00hrs **The firing resumes all around the perimeter, but this time the number of Americans participating has doubled. Spanish casualties mount and they are prevented from moving freely around their defensive perimeter.**

(iii) 09:00hrs **Cuban insurgents are placed to the north, to prevent the escape of the Spanish from the village.**

CHAFFEE

EL CANEY

BARBED WIRE

C B

D

E A

EL VISO FORT

11

10

9 **SUGARLOAF HILL**

7

8

(iv) 09:00hrs **The brigades of Gen. Ludlow on the left flank and Gen. Chaffee on the right are positioned in a semi-circle around the village. A general firefight ensues, particularly on the American left flank, which has established itself within close range of the village's southern defence line. After an hour, the volunteer regiments are pulled back into reserve, having taken substantial casualties.**

CUBAN INSURGENTS

(x) 14:00hrs **Gen. Vara del Rey notes that the capture of El Viso exposes the Spanish defensive perimeter to the south of the village. Now under pressure all along their line, the Spanish fall back to an inner defensive line in the village itself.**

(ix) 13:45hrs **The fort is captured, and the handful of surviving Spaniards retreat to the main defence line under heavy fire.**

(viii) 13:30hrs **Gen. Lawton orders the assault up the hill in his centre, the objective being El Viso. Heavy Spanish fire causes sufficient casualties to make the advance falter, but suppressive fire and an outflanking attempt using broken terrain weaken this.**

BATES

THE BATTLE FOR EL CANEY
1st July 1898 06:00–15:00hrs

What Gen. Shafter planned as a small, secondary operation turned out to be the hardest-fought engagement of the campaign. A small garrison of hopelessly outnumbered Spanish defenders held their own against a reinforced American division. Planners expected the battle to last two hours. Instead it took almost a third of the American army a whole day to capture the village.

ABOVE **A blockhouse and defence line at El Caney, looking east. The Spanish held these positions for almost a day, despite being heavily outnumbered. (National Archives)**

For around an hour, from 9:00am, the left and centre of the American line were engaged in a vicious and deadly firefight. Gen. Ludlow had his horse shot from under him, and his soldiers burrowed into the soil or crouched behind trees, trying to avoid the hail of Mauser bullets. The most intense exchange of fire was on the extreme left, where the 2nd Massachusetts Volunteer Infantry Regiment held their position astride the sunken road. Their colonel was wounded in the exchange, although overall casualties did not reflect the intensity of the fire. It appeared that for the most part, both sides tended to fire over the heads of the enemy. To inexperienced troops, the fire must have been terrifying. 'The buggers are hidden behind rocks, in weeds, in the underbrush. We can't see them, and they are shooting us to pieces' one volunteer told a reporter. The Volunteers, armed with black-powder Springfield rifles, were more of a liability than an asset and Ludlow decided to pull the regiment out of line, replacing them with two regular regiments armed with modern Krag rifles. The Massachusetts regiment was placed in reserve about 300 yards to the south-west, where they served as a blocking force which would prevent reinforcements reaching the village from Santiago.

Capron's Battery fired shell after shell into the ruins of the El Viso Fort, and also bombarded the rifle pits and trenches covering its southern side. Chaffee continued to edge his troops forward. The US 7th Infantry held ground behind and to the east of the fort, where it could cover the rear of the Spanish defences as well as the eastern side of the village itself. A withering Spanish fire prevented any further advance. The regiment was effectively pinned down until the fort was

ABOVE **A street in El Caney, looking north-east. Although many of the buildings were flimsy, a handful of stone houses and the church served as mini strongholds. (National Archives)**

neutralised. The remaining two regiments of Chaffee's brigade (the 12th and 17th Regiments) moved into position on the south-eastern slope of El Viso Hill. They found that a slight dip in the ground protected them from the worst of the Spanish fire, and the regiments lay low, preparing themselves for the inevitable assault on the fort. At around 10:00am, Gen. Ludlow ordered his men to cease firing, and they rested and smoked while badly needed ammunition supplies were brought up from the rear. The Spanish fire also slackened, as both sides prepared themselves for the renewal of the fighting. For the next three hours, only the occasional report of Spanish and American sharpshooters firing on exposed targets broke the silence. By noon the temperature was well over 90º Fahrenheit, and the humidity made the air damp and difficult to breathe.

Col. Miles was ordered to insert his brigade between those of Ludlow and Chaffee, and his troops also prepared for the assault. By noon they were in position, about 800 yards from the Spanish fort. Dead and wounded were taken to the rear. Lt. Moss of the 25th ('Negro') Regiment heard stretcher-bearers tell his men: 'Give them hell, boys. They've been doin' us dirt all morning.' At midday a message arrived at divisional headquarters from Gen. Shafter. Concerned by the delay taken in what should have been a quick and relatively easy engagement, Shafter wrote: 'I would not bother with little blockhouses. They can't harm us. Bates' Brigade and your Division and Garçia should move on the city and form the right of the line, going on Sevilla road. Line is now hotly engaged.'

The sound of the battle raging around El Caney had all but drowned out the increasing sounds of battle to the south at San Juan Hill. Shafter wanted Lawton and his attached Cuban allies to finish the job in hand and move towards the sound of the guns at San Juan. His reference to the Sevilla road was meant to be a crude indication of divisional areas. The troops of Kent's Division and the cavalry would make the main assault on the San Juan Heights, and Lawton would take the secondary objective of the extension to the main San Juan position, west and north of Kettle Hill and the blockhouse. The break in firing around El Caney gave Gen. Lawton the opportunity to size up the task ahead of him for the first time. He realised that the fortified village would be a far harder objective to capture than anyone had anticipated. Although he had the option of moving the brigades of Miles and Bates around the village and sending them towards the San Juan River to the west, he felt his two engaged brigades needed all the support they could get. All four brigades would be fed into the forthcoming attack, and Shafter and the rest of the army would have to perform as best they could without support.

At around 1:00pm, firing began again from the left, where Gen. Ludlow's brigade was ordered to open fire in support of the assault on the fort. Gen. Lawton ordered Chaffee and Miles to advance up the hill. A first line consisted of the 4th and 25th ('Negro') Regiment from Miles' brigade, with the 12th Regiment of Chaffee's brigade to their right. A second line formed from the remainder of both brigades (the 1st and 17th regiments) advanced 200 yards behind the first. The

The US 7th Infantry Regiment firing on El Caney from the north. These troops formed part of Gen. Chaffee's Brigade. Sketch by C.M. Sheldon. From Leslie's Weekly, August 1898. (Monroe County Public Library)

first 200 yards from the positions at the foot of the hill were screened by a double row of trees running alongside a small track. Beyond this lay a barbed wire fence and an open field of pineapples. Further up the hill, a belt of scrub offered a small degree of cover, but the final 400 yards would consist of an increasingly steep slope, where the knee-high sawgrass offered no cover whatsoever. Lt. Moss recalled what happened after the troops crossed the barbed wire fence: 'Ye Gods! It's raining lead! The line recoils like a mighty serpent, and then in confusion, advances again! The Spaniards now see us and pour a murderous fire into our ranks! Men are dropping everywhere … the bullets cut up the pineapples at our feet … the slaughter is awful! … How helpless, oh how helpless we feel! Our men are being shot down at our very feet, and we, their officers can do nothing for them!'

Nervous troops and officers looked towards Chaffee, who was leading the assault of the first line. Standing in the middle of the pineapple patch, he ordered that the advance was to continue. He realised that the Spanish had zeroed in their rifles on the barbed wire fence and pineapple patch, and a rapid advance could well be the only way to avoid further casualties. By this time the line had been broken into clumps of men, seeking cover wherever they could find it. A fold in the ground on the right wing of the first line offered a likely avenue of advance, and a

El Viso Fort viewed from the south, showing the approach route of the US 12th Infantry Regiment in their storming of the fortification. The photograph was taken from the edge of the pineapple patch where the Spanish fire was so severe it almost stalled the attack. (National Archives)

The stone fort at El Viso, pictured on the day after the battle for El Caney. The damage caused by artillery fire from Capron's battery was substantial. (National Archives)

company of the 12th Infantry spearheaded the way, doubled over to remain protected from the Spanish fire. Hopelessly intermingled, the remaining units of the first line also probed forward as best they could. Now within 200 yards of the enemy trenches, the Americans found themselves able to see the Spanish troops inside the fort and the surrounding rifle pits. For the first time since the advance began, the Americans were able to fire on the enemy. With fewer than 200 defenders on the hill and no fewer than 1,500 attackers in the first wave alone, the outcome was never in doubt.

'Our firing line is now no more than 150 yards from the fort, and our men are doing grand work. A general fusillading for a few minutes and then orders are given for no one but marksmen and sharpshooters to fire. Thirty or forty of these dead shots are pouring lead into every rifle pit, door, window and porthole in sight. The earth, brick and mortar are fairly flying! The Spanish are shaken and demoralised; bareheaded and

The storming of the Spanish fort of El Viso. The fort would prove to be the key to the El Caney defences. Painting by Frederic Remington. (Frederic Remington Collection)

The interior of El Viso Fort immediately after its capture. The interior apparently resembled 'a charnel house'. Sketch by C.M. Sheldon. From *Leslie's Weekly*, August 1898. (Monroe County Public Library)

without rifles, they are frantically running from their rifle pits … our men are shooting them down like dogs. A young officer is running up and down, back of the firing line and … is exclaiming; Come on men, we've got them on the run. "Remember the Maine!" Shouts a Sergeant. Four are shot down in the door of the fort. A Spaniard appears in the door … and presents … a white flag, but is shot down. Another takes up the flag, and he too falls.'

Officers managed to stop the firing, and troops moved forward to secure the small battered fort. In the lead was a journalist, James Creelman, of Hearst's *New York Journal*. In a seemingly schoolboy fit of bravado he helped spearhead the attack, and was trying to recover the fallen Spanish flag outside the fort when he was wounded. The fort interior was found to be full of dead and wounded, and the floors slippery with blood. Capt. Lee noted that the surrounding trenches were: 'floored with dead Spaniards in horribly contorted attitudes … Those killed … were all shot through the forehead, and their brains oozed out like white paint from a colour tube'. Numerous shrapnel wounds amongst the casualties in the fort bore witness to the efficiency of the gunners of Capron's Battery, and the interior walls were pock-marked with bullets, fired during the remaining minutes of the assault. A handful of Spanish prisoners surrendered, while a few others fled down the reverse slope of the hill, covered by fire from defences in the village itself.

At around 1:30pm, the situation looked grim for Gen. Vara del Rey and the remaining Spanish defenders. Retreat into the hills to the north of the village was impossible, because Cuban insurgents had blocked that avenue of retreat. Communications with Santiago were cut, and there was little hope of reinforcements reaching the garrison from the city. The Americans held El Viso, the strongest defensive point on the village perimeter, and their position now overlooked the Spanish trenches in the village. With fewer than 300 defenders remaining and able to fight, the Spanish faced odds of about 20 to 1. There was no doubt that the

Spanish prisoners captured after the battle at El Caney. Most defenders were either killed or wounded, and the dead included the local commander Gen. Vara del Ray and his two sons. (National Archives)

Americans would prevail. As well as the immediate situation in the village, Gen. del Rey was by now aware that the Americans were also assaulting San Juan Heights, and were directly threatening Santiago itself. He realised that his force had caused a substantial disruption to the American plan of attack, and the division facing him would be unable to reinforce the main American assault to the south. By denying Shafter over one third of his army, he might buy enough time for the Spanish to reinforce the city and repel the main American attack. He decided to continue the unequal fight.

The Americans milling around on top of El Viso Hill had little opportunity to rest on their laurels. A heavy fire opened up from the village, the new defensive line centred on a blockhouse on the south-eastern corner. From there a line of trenches and wire ran west to the south-western corner of the village, where another blockhouse served to anchor the Spanish position. To the north of this, along the western edge of the village, Spanish marksmen in fortified houses continued to fire on Ludlow's troops in the sunken road. The 2nd Brigade continued to fire on the Spanish positions, and covered by this fusillade, men from the remaining two brigades ran down the reverse slope of the hill and along a crest line running parallel to the village. Regiments were jumbled together, and discipline seemed to have been lost completely. This did remove many of the men from the exposed hilltop and brought them into a position where they could pour fire down from the crest on the nearest blockhouse, 200 yards to the west. One American officer records the incident:

'As long as we remain in our present position, we can accomplish but little, as the walls of the blockhouse are impervious to our bullets. It is therefore decided to rush forward and change direction to our left, thus gaining a position facing, and slightly above the blockhouse … The line is now occupying its new position … some of our men are shooting into the town, and others are shooting down through the roof of the blockhouse … the Spanish are falling.'

This enfilading fire forced the defenders to abandon the blockhouse, and the Spanish withdrew from their line along the edge of the village, taking up a last stand in the central and western part of El Caney. A handful of defenders still held the western blockhouse and the stone church, and buildings between them were loopholed for defence. Gen. del Rey was reportedly seen on horseback, exhorting his men to give one final effort. As Ludlow's men advanced to capture the abandoned Spanish forward positions, they were subjected to steady rifle fire from the village itself. With the rest of the division closing in on the village centre from the east, sheer weight of numbers and lack of ammunition on the part of the defenders brought resistance to a bloody end. A hail of shots was fired on the Spanish positions, and by 3:00pm the resistance was over.

Gen. Joaquin Vara del Rey was killed in the final minutes of the action as he directed the last stand from the plaza in front of the church. Wounded in the legs, he was being placed on a stretcher when he was

struck in the head. He died instantly, and with him went the Spanish will to continue the bloody fight. His two sons, serving as aides, were also killed in the action. His second-in-command, Lt.Col. Punet, ordered that the surviving defenders should break out to the north-west, to avoid capture. With just over 100 men left unwounded, Punet's action succeeded, and slipping round the flank of Ludlow's brigade, over 80 men made it back to Santiago. Of the 520 Spanish defenders, 235 had been killed and a further 120 were taken prisoner.

The British Capt. Lee watched the American troops attack the Spanish blockhouse in the final assault on the village perimeter. Turning to an American officer, he asked: 'Is it customary with you to assault blockhouses and rifle pits before they have been searched by artillery?' 'Not always' was the embarrassed reply. A thoroughly professional defence had been overcome by weight of numbers and bravado. Lack of planning, reconnaissance and experience on the part of Gen. Lawton and Gen. Shafter caused needless American casualties in what was the bloodiest engagement of the campaign. American losses were 81 men killed, including four officers. A further 360 were wounded, and the subsequent lack of medical attention meant that many wounds would prove fatal. In fact, around 10 per cent of the effective strength of Lawton's division was lost in what was meant to be a simple clearing operation. Vara del Rey also achieved his goal of preventing Lawton's troops from reinforcing Shafter. After a somewhat half-hearted probe at dusk towards the Ducrot House and Santiago, Lawton decided not to risk his bloodied division in a night attack in unfamiliar terrain. He simply retraced his steps back to Marianage and El Pozo and did not

DAVID RICKMAN

GRIMES'S BATTERY OPENING FIRE ON THE SPANISH BLOCKHOUSE

At 8:20am on the morning of 1 July 1898, the battery on El Pozo Hill shattered the silence by starting its bombardment of the Spanish blockhouse on the neighbouring San Juan Hill. The Spanish quickly replied with counter-battery fire, killing a number of troops passing along the road near the American battery position. A cluster of foreign military observers, staff officers and war correspondents who were watching the bombardment also hastily ran for cover: it was an almost comic start to what would be a bloody day. The battery was armed with four 3.2 in. Quick Firing Field Guns, considered obsolete by most foreign observers. They used black-powder cartridges to propel their shells, and these produced thick clouds of smoke, which betrayed the gun position to the Spanish. Spanish artillery pieces used smokeless powder, which reduced the chances of effective counter-battery fire. The bombardment was fired at a range of just over a mile, and lasted approximately 30 minutes. The fourth round fired hit the roof of the blockhouse, and after that the bombardment was on target and effective, despite the obvious obsolescence of the guns. A Lack of ammunition prevented the battery continuing the action, a supply error typical of the logistical difficulties that dogged the campaign.

reach San Juan Heights until just before noon on the following day. A Spanish officer said of the action: 'the Americans it must be acknowledged, fought that day with truly admirable courage and spirit … but they met heroes'.

THE APPROACH MARCH

At around 4:00am, the main army stirred itself and prepared a breakfast of hardtack and coffee. Frederic Remington, the artist, watched the horses of Grimes's four-gun battery pull the guns onto El Pozo Hill, from where they could shell the Heights. The rest of the army, backed up on the Sevilla road, prepared to march into battle. As Pvt. Post of the 71st New York Volunteer Regiment advanced, he heard Capron's guns open up on El Caney, four miles to the north, and 'for the first time it dawned on us that there might be fighting ahead'. His regiment passed the mounted figures of William Randolph Hearst and *New York Journal* correspondent James Creelman, who were watching the troops. 'Hey Willie!' cried the troops. 'Good luck!' responded the news magnate who had done more than anyone else to start the war that was about to reach its climax; 'Boys, good luck be with you.'

Gen. Kent arrived on El Pozo Hill just as Grimes's battery was deploying, watched by a crowd of staff officers, military attachés and journalists. Lt.Col. McClerland briefed him and showed him the Heights. On the left of the main ridge, marked on the map as 'San Juan Hill', sat a blockhouse with a red tile roof. Once his column reached the meadow he was to deploy to the left of the road, then attack it. Gen. Sumner's dismounted cavalry would deploy to the right of the road, attack the outlying Kettle Hill, then the main ridge of San Juan Heights behind it. As he waited for the battle to start Kent chatted to Maj. John Jacob Astor, staff officer and multi-millionaire. The El Caney action had been raging for almost two hours, so it was presumed to be drawing to a close. The frontal assault was timed to coincide with the reinforcements of Lawton's division arriving from

The observation balloon that drew heavy Spanish rifle fire onto the troops strung out below it on the road leading to Bloody Ford: it was later shot down there. (National Archives)

Capt. Grimes's battery on El Pozo Hill pictured opening fire on the Spanish blockhouse on San Juan Hill. The Spanish would return fire within seconds of the photograph being taken. (National Archives)

El Caney. Lt.Col. McClerland looked at his watch, decided it was time to start, and ordered Capt. Grimes to open fire. It was almost exactly 8:20am.

The first 3.2 in. gun fired amid a cloud of black powder, and its shell overshot the blockhouse: the following two did likewise. With the fourth round, though, the battery found its mark, scoring a hit on the blockhouse roof and raising a cheer from the observers. The newspaper artist Howard Chandler Christy remembered that 'a shell went through the roof and exploded, covering itself in a reddish smoke and throwing pieces of tile and cement into the air'. The other guns ranged in and bombarded the blockhouse and the surrounding trenches.

Col. Wood turned to Lt.Col. Roosevelt and, eyeing the crowd of onlookers behind the guns, remarked that there would be hell to pay if the Spanish returned fire. As he spoke, two Krupp shells whistled overhead and exploded behind them on El Pozo plantation itself. A chunk of shrapnel hit Roosevelt's wrist 'raising a bump about as big as a hickory nut'. Others weren't as lucky. The salvo landed amongst a huddle of Cuban insurgents and waiting Rough Riders, killing and wounding several soldiers. The observers ran for cover, leaving the gunners to continue their bombardment alone. Grimes fired for another 30 minutes then ceased, awaiting ammunition and orders.

Sumner's men, followed by those of Kent's division, continued up the Camino Real. Just past El Pozo, the muddy road narrowed, forcing the men to march two abreast rather than in a column of fours. Continuous halts made the approach march seem interminable, but once within a mile of the San Juan River, the head of the column came under heavy fire. Pvt. Post and the 71st New York Volunteers heard the firecracker popping of the Mausers, and an occasional buzz as a bullet hit a tree. He was under fire at last: 'I felt a tenseness in my throat, a dryness that was not a thirst, and little chilly surges in my stomach.'

The Spanish were familiar with the terrain, and knew where the road paralleled the Aguadores River as it snaked through the jungle. They had marked the range and fired repeated volleys into the jungle, concentrating on the points where the road crossed streams, which would create bottlenecks. Richard Harding Davis likened the terrain to a place 'where cattle are chased into the chutes of the Chicago cattle-pen'. Spanish sharpshooters added to the hail of bullets by sniping at the American soldiers from both sides of the trail. To add to the confusion, the Signal Corps had inflated an observation balloon, and, tethered to a wagon, it accompanied the troops as they marched down the trail. It also served as a perfect range marker for the Spanish. 'Huge, fat, yellow, quivering', it drew heavy fire, and Maj. Maxwell commanding the balloon detachment quickly became the most unpopular man in the army.

Roosevelt was furious that it was risking the lives of his men. Crossing the San Juan River, he was ordered by McClernand to branch to the right, head upstream, then wait for orders. 'I promptly hurried my men across, for the fire was getting hot, and the captive balloon to the horror of everybody, was coming down to the ford.' Frederic Remington reached the river ford and abandoned his horse as the bullets whistled around him. 'A man came, stooping over, with his arms drawn up, and hands flapping downward at the wrists. That is the way with all people when they are shot through the body, because they want to hold the torso steady, because if they don't it hurts.' Lt. John Pershing ('Black Jack') of the 10th Cavalry, a 'Negro' regiment, remembered reaching the ford just as the bullet-shredded remains of the balloon collapsed into the river to their right. 'We were posted for a time in the bed of the stream, directly under the balloon, and stood in water to our waists awaiting orders to deploy.' Gen. Wheeler had risen from his sickbed, and the old Confederate cavalryman sat on his horse in the middle of the river, oblivious to the bullets slapping the water around him. Pershing saluted him as a piece of shrapnel ploughed into the water between them. Wheeler returned the salute and observed that: 'The shelling seems quite lively'.

As the 71st New York moved towards the ford, Pvt. Post noticed that 'the trail underfoot was slippery with mud. It was mud made by the blood of the dead and the wounded, for there had been no showers that day. The trail on either side was lined with the feet of fallen men'. Over 400 men were killed and wounded at the ford (renamed 'the Bloody Ford') and on the jungle track leading towards it. Apart from the artillery, the troops still hadn't been able to return the fire. Davis later wrote that 'Military blunders had brought 7,000 American soldiers into a chute of death'. Troops were log-jammed back up the trail from the ford, and subjected to constant fire. As units filed over the ford and deployed along the edge of its banks, the firing continued unabated, but at least the riverbank provided a small degree of protection from the Spanish rifles. Before it was brought down, the observation balloon had reported that a trail was seen branching off from the Camino Real before the ford and emerging at the river further to the south. Gen. Kent sent the next regiment, which happened to be the 71st, down the new track in an effort to relieve the log-jam. The rest of the army lay in the river bed or along the trail and awaited orders. As Davis recalled: 'Men gasped on their backs, like fishes in the bottom of a boat ... their tongues sticking out and their eyes rolling. All through this the volleys from the rifle pits sputtered and rattled, and the bullets sang continuously like the wind through the rigging in a gale ... and still no order came from Gen. Shafter.' It was now well past noon, and the leading troops had been pinned down in the river bed for over an hour. Roosevelt and the Rough Riders lay to the right of the American line along the bed, facing the Spanish outpost in the refinery on Kettle Hill. Beside them were the other troops of Wood's brigade (the 1st and 10th Cavalry). As 'Mauser bullets drove in sheets through the trees' which lined the bank, Roosevelt sent repeated requests for orders to Wood and Sumner. One of his messengers was even killed in front of him as he waited. Casualties amongst the Rough Riders were mounting, and included Capt. 'Bucky' O'Neill, hero of Las Guasimas. Roosevelt recalls that he was about to conclude that in the absence of orders he had better 'march towards the guns', when a lieutenant rode up with the 'welcome command' to advance and support the regulars in an assault on the hills. This meant a direct attack on Kettle Hill. Roosevelt summed up what happened next in the phrase he called 'My crowded hour'. It was 1:05pm.

Troops of the US 16th Infantry waiting in the riverbank of the San Juan River for the order to advance. Most US casualties were inflicted during this pause in the battle. (Library of Congress)

The Rough Riders waiting for orders to advance on Kettle Hill. The troops are shown being subjected to heavy fire. This was the period when Capt. 'Bucky' O'Neill was killed. Drawing by Frederic Remington. (Frederic Remington Collection)

THE ROUGH RIDERS'
CHARGE AT KETTLE HILL

Roosevelt ordered his regiment forward, noticing that, 'always, when men have been lying down under cover for some time, and are required to advance, there is a little hesitation'. They passed the prone figures of the regular cavalrymen, who had not yet received orders to advance, and who were positioned in front of the volunteers. Roosevelt announced that 'the thing to do was to try to rush the entrenchments', but the regular cavalry officers wanted none of it. 'Then let my men through, Sir' responded Roosevelt. As they advanced, the cavalrymen leaped up and joined them. Roosevelt noted to his left: 'the whole line, tired of waiting, and eager to close with the enemy … slipped the leash at almost the same moment … by this time we were all in the spirit of the thing and greatly excited by the charge, the men cheering and running forward between shots'. In reality, a conference of officers had just decided to order the whole line to advance and messengers had passed down the line. All along the line, regiments picked themselves up and moved ahead.

The blockhouse on San Juan Hill, seen from the Bloody Ford. Parker's Gatling guns took up a position 50 yards forward of the camera position when they opened fire on the Spanish blockhouse. (National Archives)

At Kettle Hill, elements of the three cavalry regiments of Wood's brigade scrambled over a barbed wire fence and charged up the hill towards the refinery, now only 300 yards away. To the right of the line, the Rough Riders were the first to charge. They were joined by the 10th and then the 1st Cavalry, flanked on their left by the 9th, followed by the 6th and the 3rd Cavalry regiments. The first wave therefore consisted of Buffalo Soldiers and Rough Riders. An officer ordered the troops to dress ranks on the colours, but it was too late to establish an orderly line as the volunteers threw discipline to the wind and charged headlong up the hill. All the regulars could do was to join them. A dip protected the troops from the worst of the Spanish fire until they reached the military crest about 100 yards from the Spanish rifle pits. A military attaché turned to Steven Crane, who was watching from the river, saying; 'It's plucky you know! By Gawd it's plucky! But they can't do it!' Davis saw that: 'There were so few of them. One's instinct was to call to them to come back. You felt that someone had blundered and that these few men were blindly following out some madman's mad order'. Further to the left, Crane watched the men of Hawkins' brigade charge towards the blockhouse. Someone yelled: 'By God, there go our boys up the hill! … Yes, up the hill … It was the best moment of anybody's life!' There was no turning back now.

View from the barbed wire at the foot of Kettle Hill, looking towards the Rough Riders' positions along the San Juan River. Roosevelt charged from the trees, past the camera and up the hill beyond. The Buffalo Soldiers were deployed in the grass in front of the tree line. (National Archives)

On his horse Texas, Roosevelt galloped ahead of his men towards the refinery buildings at the top of Kettle Hill, but 40 yards from the crest, Texas ran into a second barbed wire fence and was wounded. The two cavalry brigades were intermingled by now. The guidon bearer of the 3rd Cavalry fell, and a soldier of the 10th took up the flag. Roosevelt dismounted and continued over the wire followed by his orderly, Henry Bardshar. They were now less than 50 yards from the crest. Fortunately for the impetuous Roosevelt, the Spanish were not as resolute as the defenders at El Caney. As the Americans approached, the defenders began abandoning the position and fleeing back down the reverse slope of the hill and up the slope of San Juan Heights beyond. The guidon bearer of the 10th Cavalry planted his standard in the Spanish trench, followed by the standard bearer of the Rough Riders. Following behind, Remington felt the rain of Mauser bullets slacken and heard a cheer. Looking up he saw the Buffalo Soldiers' flag sticking in the Spanish parapet. American cavalrymen, both black and white, regular and volunteer were crowded together at the top of Kettle Hill, making a perfect target for Spanish marksmen firing from the Heights themselves. Their officers tried to form them into some kind of firing line, and the men returned fire to the west and to the south-west, towards the blockhouse. As the dismounted cavalrymen flopped down on the crest of Kettle Hill, they had a perfect view of the assault on San Juan Hill.

THE CHARGE UP SAN JUAN HILL

In front of Gen. Kent's division crouched in the river bed was a line of trees, from which a barbed wire fence was strung. Beyond it lay 300 yards of open meadow, between the river and the foot of the Heights. The

Lt. Parker's Gatling guns firing in support of the attack up San Juan Hill. Their fire support was the turning point of the battle. Drawing by Charles J. Post of the 71st NY Infantry. (Charles J. Post Collection)

THE BATTLE OF SAN JUAN HILL (1 JULY 1898): THE AMERICAN DEPLOYMENT

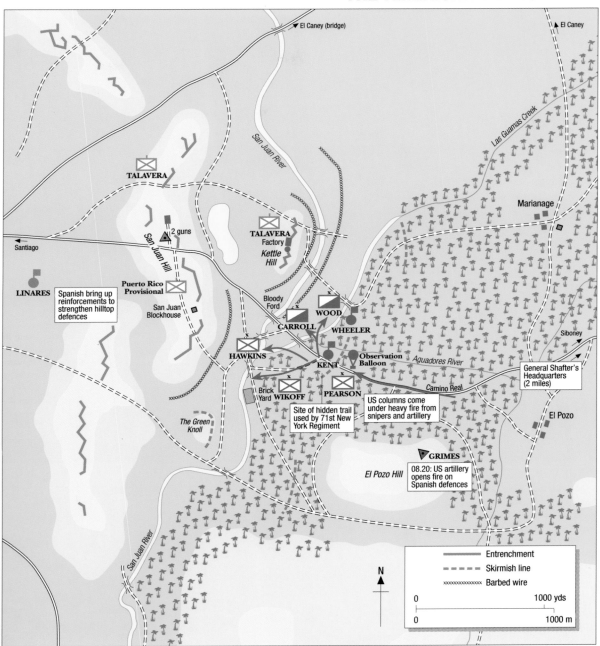

El Caney (bridge)

El Caney

TALAVERA

San Juan River

Las Guamas Creek

Marianage

2 guns

Santiago

San Juan Hill

TALAVERA
Factory
Kettle
Hill

LINARES

Spanish bring up
reinforcements to
strengthen hilltop
defences

Puerto Rico
Provisional

San Juan
Blockhouse

Bloody
Ford

WOOD

CARROLL

WHEELER

Siboney

HAWKINS

KENT

Observation
Balloon

Aguadores River

General Shafter's
Headquarters
(2 miles)

Brick
Yard WIKOFF

PEARSON

Camino Real

The Green
Knoll

Site of hidden trail
used by 71st New
York Regiment

US columns come
under heavy fire from
snipers and artillery

El Pozo

GRIMES

El Pozo Hill

08.20: US artillery
opens fire on
Spanish defences

N

	Entrenchment
	Skirmish line
xxxxxxxxxxxx	Barbed wire

0   1000 yds

0   1000 m

The principal Spanish defensive line before Santiago was along the ridge of San Juan Heights. The anchor was the blockhouse near its southern end, and this would be the focus of the American attack when it came. The ridge was protected by a forward position on Kettle Hill, and by lines of barbed wire on its eastern approaches. In the jungle beyond the San Juan River, Spanish sharpshooters were poised to snipe at the advancing Americans. Gen. Linares and Spanish reinforcements were sited a half-mile to the rear at Fort Canovar. As Grimes's battery opened fire on the blockhouse at 8:20am, the head of the column was passing El Pozo Hill. It soon came under heavy Spanish fire, and an accompanying observation balloon only served to give the Spanish a ranging marker. As the Cavalry Division reached Bloody Ford it deployed to the north-east, along the bank of the San Juan River. Kent's division deployed to the left, facing the blockhouse. The troops would now wait under constant fire while they waited for orders to attack.

RIGHT **The San Juan blockhouse and ruined barrack outbuildings, pictured after the battle. This was the linchpin of the Spanish position on San Juan Heights. (National Archives)**

ABOVE **The attack on the San Juan blockhouse, a rare photo taken by a man accompanying Hawkins' brigade. The ascending infantry can just be made out on the right. (National Archives)**

Americans tried to return the Spanish fire, but with little effect: the Spanish were too well dug in. The only way to dislodge them was by a frontal assault: in fact, faced with this prospect, the Spanish had reinforced their position. The troops on the Heights were from the 1st Provisional Battalion of Puerto Rico. They were joined by troops from the 1st Talavera Peninsular Battalion, as well as volunteers from the city. Gen. Linares himself joined his troops in the front line, near the blockhouse. Around 1,000 Spanish soldiers and two guns now waited on the Heights. The weight of fire from the Spanish positions was taking its toll and American casualties were mounting: among these was Col. Wikoff, commanding Kent's 3rd Brigade. Two regimental commanders were also killed as they waited at the riverbank. Aides rode back to Shafter to try to get him to order an advance, but no message ever reached the front line. The decision to advance would have to be made by the men on the spot. A group of officers waited for orders on the Camino Real, above the Bloody Ford. Gen. Sumner, Gen. Kent, several brigadiers and Lt. Miley, Gen. Shafter's aide, held an impromptu conference. In the end it was the lieutenant as Shafter's representative who made the decision. Shortly after 1.00pm, he declared that: 'the Heights must be taken at all costs'. The meeting broke up and couriers raced to take the message to attack to the waiting regimental commanders.

The attack on the Heights started in the centre of the American line, where Gen. Hawkins and his brigade faced the Spanish blockhouse, to the left of the Camino Real. Once over the fence and out of the tree line along the river the ground was flat for 300 yards before the base of the Heights rose out of the valley floor. As the line advanced, it came under heavy fire, and was pinned down in the long grass of the valley floor. Further down the line, most of the troops were still in the tree line along the river or in the jungle behind it. At around 1.15pm, the attackers heard a drumming sound, 'like a coffee grinder'. Fear of Spanish machine guns was replaced by elation, when the Americans worked out that the sound came from their own Gatling guns. Lt. Parker and his four Gatlings had taken up a position in front of the Bloody Ford and opened up a heavy suppressive fire on the Spanish positions around the blockhouse. At a range of just under 700 yards, the Gatlings fired for eight minutes, and thousands of rounds swept over the Spanish positions. This fire proved to be the decisive moment of the battle. At around 1.20pm, as the Gatlings and fire from Kettle Hill pinned down the Spanish defenders on the Heights, Lt. Jules G. Ord of the 6th Infantry jumped to his feet, yelling: 'Come on! We can't stop here!' The rest of Hawkins' brigade resumed the attack, spearheaded by the 6th and 16th Infantry regiments. Once at the foot of the Heights, they discovered that the Spanish had committed a cardinal military sin: they had dug their trenches on the topographical crest of the Heights, and not the 'military crest'. The 'military crest' is a line below the actual crest which offers the defenders an unrestricted field of fire all the way to the base of the hill. By lining the topographical crest, the Spanish created 'dead ground' for most of the way up the hill, where the topography shielded the attackers from Spanish bullets. Once at the base of the hill, the attackers would be safe until they approached the top. As the troops reached the top, the supporting fire from Kettle Hill and the Gatlings ceased, and at around 1.28pm, the Americans reached the Spanish

trenches. The Gatling fire had broken the resolve of the defenders, and most were fleeing back towards Santiago. A few fought on, and Lt. Ord was killed on the parapet of the Spanish trench. Within a few minutes it was all over, and the blockhouse was in American hands.

Richard Harding Davis watched the troops storm the hill. 'They had no glittering bayonets, they were not massed in regular array. There were a few men in advance, bunched together and creeping up a steep, sunny hill, the top of which roared and crashed with flame ... Behind the first few, spread out like a fan, were single lines of men, slipping and scrambling in the smooth grass, moving with difficulty ...

THE CHARGE OF THE
ROUGH RIDERS UP KETTLE HILL
The image that endured in public imagination from the campaign was the charge of Teddy Roosevelt and his Rough Riders up San Juan Hill. In reality, although the event was a crucial element of the American victory, it formed only one part of a larger engagement. Instead of San Juan Hill, the Rough Riders charged up Kettle Hill, a smaller feature in front of San Juan Heights. San Juan Hill was the name given to the end of the Heights where the Spanish blockhouse was sited. Also, although Roosevelt and the Rough Riders initiated the charge up Kettle Hill, they were accompanied by elements of several other regiments, most notably the Buffalo Soldiers of the 9th and 10th

DAVID
RICKMAN

('Negro') US Cavalry Regiments. Contrary to many popular depictions, all the cavalrymen charged up the hill on foot. The only mounted figures were a handful of officers, including Roosevelt himself, who was on his horse Texas. The charge was carried out almost simultaneously along the whole American front line, with the Rough Riders on the right flank of the advance. Where the main attack on the Heights was temporarily stalled, the cavalrymen took Kettle Hill in the first assault. Roosevelt was a consummate politician, and the correspondents he courted so carefully highlighted his obvious courage in such a way that he became the linchpin of the battle. This undoubtedly also helped his future electoral prospects.

a thin blue line that kept creeping higher and higher up the hill.'

When Gen. Sumner and Col. Wood reached the top of Kettle Hill, Roosevelt asked for permission to continue the advance to the second objective, the northern spur of San Juan Heights. Sumner agreed, and Roosevelt led the jumbled bulk of several cavalry regiments now on the hill down the other side. Around 800 cavalrymen charged for a second time, as the remainder of the division on Kettle Hill fired in support. As was the case with the blockhouse, this supporting fire was crucial in pinning down the heavily outnumbered defenders.

ABOVE **The death of Lt. Ord, as US troops reach the Spanish breastworks on San Juan Hill. Drawing by Charles J. Post of the 71st NY Infantry. It was Ord who precipitated the final charge. (Charles J. Post Collection)**

RIGHT **The rear of San Juan Hill, seen from the crest of Kettle Hill in a photo taken after the battle. The San Juan blockhouse is on the left edge of the crest. The Cavalry Division later set up camp on this reverse slope, to reduce casualties from stray Spanish fire. (National Archives)**

LEFT **The charge up San Juan Hill; a stylised version, one of many to appear in American publications (many of the artists commissioned to produce these were not even present). Drawing by William J. Glackens. From *McClure's Magazine*, October 1898. (Monroe County Public Library)**

In this section of the Spanish line, barely 200 men faced 2,000 American cavalrymen. The attackers moved around the sides of a small lake, and swarmed up the steep slope on the other side. Fortunately, this sector of the Heights was sparsely defended, and the slope was too steep to let the Spaniards fire on the cavalrymen until they reached their trenches. At that point most of the Spanish decided that they were hopelessly outnumbered and retreated back towards Santiago. A handful remained to contest the crest. Two fired on Roosevelt from ten yards away but missed. 'I closed in and fired twice, missing the first and killing the second. My revolver was from the sunken battleship *Maine* ... Most of the fallen had little holes in their heads from which their brains were oozing.' Capt. Lee and Lt.Col. Roosevelt had both observed the same phenomenon: the Spanish heads exposed above the rifle pits were the only target for the American infantrymen, so head wounds were the predominant form of injury. It also attested to the accuracy of the Krag rifle.

The cavalrymen dug in on the crest. Gen. Sumner brought up the remainder of the division and strung it out along the ridge to the left and right of Roosevelt's position. A Spanish counterattack was expected, and the exhausted troopers were in no fit state to meet it. An hour later, Sumner, Wood and Roosevelt were joined in the former Spanish

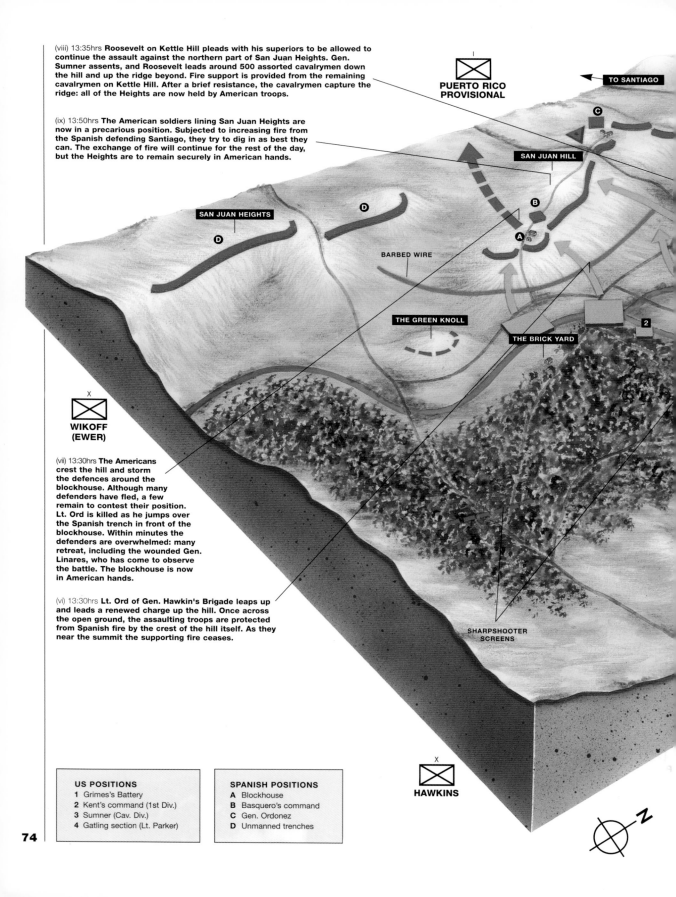

(viii) 13:35hrs **Roosevelt on Kettle Hill pleads with his superiors to be allowed to continue the assault against the northern part of San Juan Heights. Gen. Sumner assents, and Roosevelt leads around 500 assorted cavalrymen down the hill and up the ridge beyond. Fire support is provided from the remaining cavalrymen on Kettle Hill. After a brief resistance, the cavalrymen capture the ridge: all of the Heights are now held by American troops.**

(ix) 13:50hrs **The American soldiers lining San Juan Heights are now in a precarious position. Subjected to increasing fire from the Spanish defending Santiago, they try to dig in as best they can. The exchange of fire will continue for the rest of the day, but the Heights are to remain securely in American hands.**

PUERTO RICO PROVISIONAL

TO SANTIAGO

C

SAN JUAN HILL

B

SAN JUAN HEIGHTS

D

D

A

BARBED WIRE

THE GREEN KNOLL

THE BRICK YARD

2

WIKOFF (EWER)

(vii) 13:30hrs **The Americans crest the hill and storm the defences around the blockhouse. Although many defenders have fled, a few remain to contest their position. Lt. Ord is killed as he jumps over the Spanish trench in front of the blockhouse. Within minutes the defenders are overwhelmed: many retreat, including the wounded Gen. Linares, who has come to observe the battle. The blockhouse is now in American hands.**

(vi) 13:30hrs **Lt. Ord of Gen. Hawkin's Brigade leaps up and leads a renewed charge up the hill. Once across the open ground, the assaulting troops are protected from Spanish fire by the crest of the hill itself. As they near the summit the supporting fire ceases.**

SHARPSHOOTER SCREENS

HAWKINS

US POSITIONS
1 Grimes's Battery
2 Kent's command (1st Div.)
3 Sumner (Cav. Div.)
4 Gatling section (Lt. Parker)

SPANISH POSITIONS
A Blockhouse
B Basquero's command
C Gen. Ordonez
D Unmanned trenches

N

74

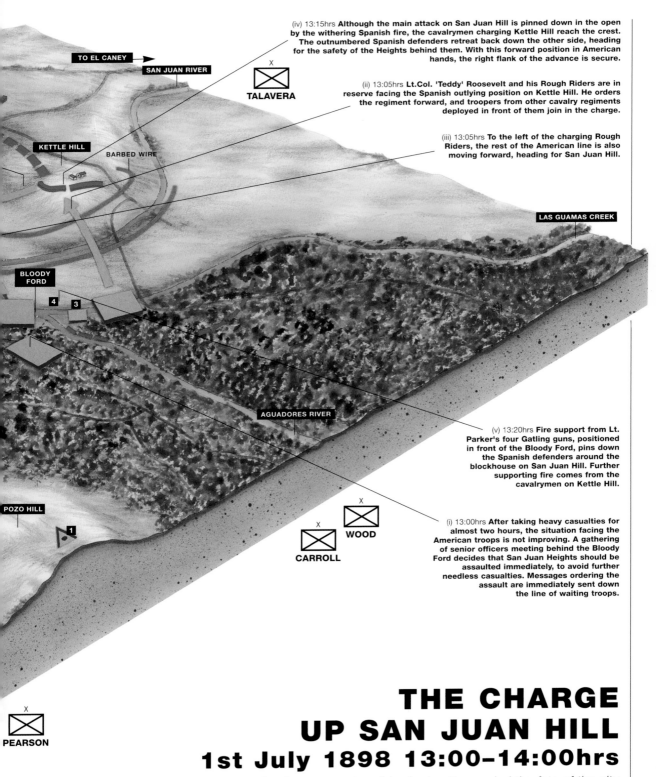

(iv) 13:15hrs Although the main attack on San Juan Hill is pinned down in the open by the withering Spanish fire, the cavalrymen charging Kettle Hill reach the crest. The outnumbered Spanish defenders retreat back down the other side, heading for the safety of the Heights behind them. With this forward position in American hands, the right flank of the advance is secure.

(ii) 13:05hrs Lt.Col. 'Teddy' Roosevelt and his Rough Riders are in reserve facing the Spanish outlying position on Kettle Hill. He orders the regiment forward, and troopers from other cavalry regiments deployed in front of them join in the charge.

(iii) 13:05hrs To the left of the charging Rough Riders, the rest of the American line is also moving forward, heading for San Juan Hill.

(v) 13:20hrs Fire support from Lt. Parker's four Gatling guns, positioned in front of the Bloody Ford, pins down the Spanish defenders around the blockhouse on San Juan Hill. Further supporting fire comes from the cavalrymen on Kettle Hill.

(i) 13:00hrs After taking heavy casualties for almost two hours, the situation facing the American troops is not improving. A gathering of senior officers meeting behind the Bloody Ford decides that San Juan Heights should be assaulted immediately, to avoid further needless casualties. Messages ordering the assault are immediately sent down the line of waiting troops.

TO EL CANEY

SAN JUAN RIVER

TALAVERA

KETTLE HILL

BARBED WIRE

LAS GUAMAS CREEK

BLOODY FORD

4 3

AGUADORES RIVER

POZO HILL

1

WOOD

CARROLL

PEARSON

THE CHARGE UP SAN JUAN HILL
1st July 1898 13:00–14:00hrs

The climax of the Santiago campaign, this short action sealed the fate of the city and of the Spanish naval squadron sheltering in its harbour. 'Teddy' Roosevelt later described the events following his receipt of the order to charge as 'My crowded hour'.

ABOVE **The San Juan blockhouse pictured soon after its capture. The damage caused by the barrage from Grimes's and Parker's batteries is clearly seen. Drawing by Charles J. Post of the 71st NY Infantry. (Charles J. Post Collection)**

trenches by a group of journalists, including Stephen Crane, Frederic Remington and Richard Harding Davis. Together they peered over the crest towards Santiago. Spanish rifle and artillery fire still swept the ridge, and the situation seemed precarious. Crane, seemingly impervious, walked along the crest, smoking a pipe. Davis yelled: 'You're not impressing anyone by doing that, Crane', and stung by the insinuation of being a poseur, Crane returned to the trench. Conditions were still desperate and the line was thinly held. As Harding noted: 'They were seldom more than a company at any one spot, and there were bare spaces from 100 to 200 yards apart held by only a dozen men. The position was painfully reminiscent of Humpty-Dumpty on the wall.' As night fell, the Americans felt as if they were clinging to the ridge by their fingernails.

Casualties were heavy. In the battles at El Caney and San Juan, the Americans lost over 200 men killed, and over 1,100 wounded. 125 of those killed had died at San Juan. These losses amounted to about 10 per cent of the total force available to Gen. Shafter. The Spanish lost 215 killed and 375 wounded most of whom became prisoners of war. Gen. Linares was wounded in the action, and Gen. Toral, who assumed

The battleship USS *Oregon*, pictured in her pre-war white paint scheme. She joined her sister ships the *Indiana* and *Massachusetts* at Key West in time to participate in the campaign after a marathon voyage from the US Pacific coast. (Library of Congress)

command of the defenders, was unable to organise a counterattack. In the end, it slowly dawned on everyone that the Americans had gained an enormous strategic advantage. When Lawton's men joined the defenders the next day, and helped secure the American positions, the chance for the Spanish to launch a successful counterattack evaporated. Once heavy guns could be brought up, the Americans could fire on the town below them. More importantly, the Spanish squadron whose arrival in Santiago had been the cause of the war, would also lie at the mercy of the American guns. That night, Admiral Cervera recalled the 1,000 sailors he had landed to bolster the defences of the city. He had a choice; either to try to run from the American blockade – or remain in the harbour and be sunk.

LEFT **'Teddy' Roosevelt and the Rough Riders pictured on San Juan Heights in the days after the battle. This classic photograph by William Dinwiddie is the most widely recognised image of the war. (Library of Congress)**

AFTERMATH

THE NAVAL BATTLE OF SANTIAGO

After San Juan Hill was captured on 1 July 1898, the Spanish options were limited. To remain in harbour was to risk being destroyed at anchor by army artillery batteries: to try to break through the American blockade was to invite certain destruction. The four Spanish cruisers and two destroyers were also in poor shape. The *Cristobal Colon* lacked her main armament, the *Vizcaya* had a fouled bottom, and both she and the *Almirante Oquendo* had a number of inoperable secondary guns. Also, 80 per cent of the ammunition carried was defective. If the badly prepared Spanish cruisers took on the larger force of American battleships, they would be destroyed. The Spanish hoped to use the flagship cruiser, *Infanta Maria Teresa*, to ram the fastest American

THE NAVAL BATTLE OF SANTIAGO (3 JULY 1898)

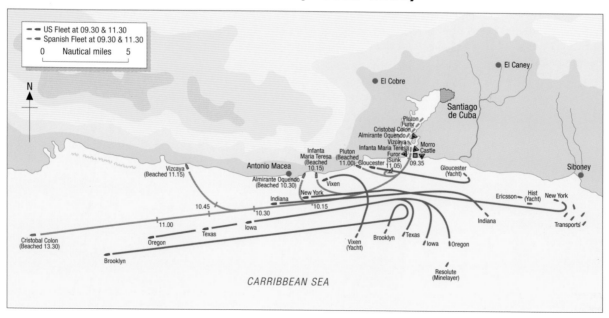

The Spanish naval squadron of four cruisers and two destroyers had brought the war to Santiago by sheltering in the port. The capture of San Juan Heights made its destruction inevitable if it remained there. Admiral Cervera decided to sortie, attempting to run through the US naval blockade. Admiral Sampson in the *New York* was several miles to the east when the Spanish emerged, and he spent the morning trying to catch up with the battle. Admiral Schley ordered the American ships to close in and give chase. A heavy exchange of salvoes began, and the heavier and more accurate American guns began to find their targets. One by one the Spanish cruisers were hit repeatedly, then forced to run for the shore and beach themselves. By 11:30am only the *Cristobal Colon* remained afloat: it would be chased for another two hours before sharing the fate of its consorts.

THE SIEGE OF SANTIAGO (2 JULY TO 13 JULY 1898)

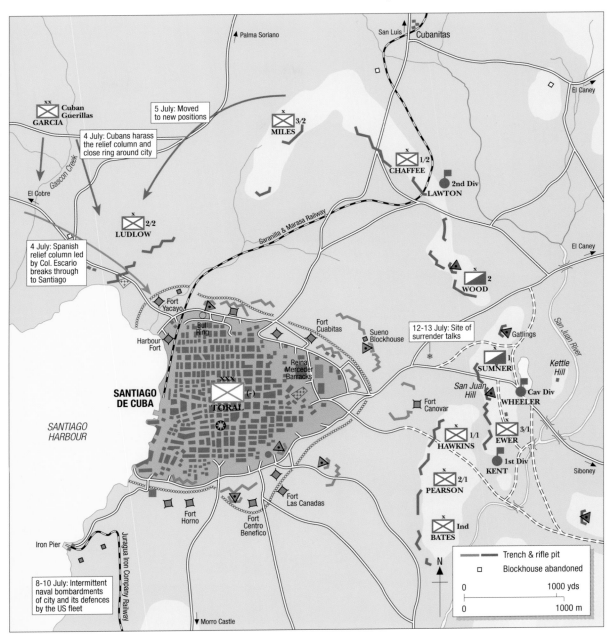

Cuban Guerillas — GARCIA

5 July: Moved to new positions

4 July: Cubans harass the relief column and close ring around city

3/2 — MILES

1/2 — CHAFFEE

2nd Div — LAWTON

2/2 — LUDLOW

4 July: Spanish relief column led by Col. Escario breaks through to Santiago

2 — WOOD

12-13 July: Site of surrender talks

Gatlings

1 — SUMNER

Cav Div — WHEELER

Kettle Hill

San Juan Hill

1/1 — HAWKINS

3/1 — EWER

1st Div — KENT

2/1 — PEARSON

Ind — BATES

SANTIAGO DE CUBA — TORAL

SANTIAGO HARBOUR

Fort Yacayo

Bull Ring

Harbour Fort

Reina Merceder Barracks

Fort Cuabitas

Sueno Blockhouse

Fort Canovar

Fort Horno

Fort Centro Benefico

Fort Las Canadas

Iron Pier

8-10 July: Intermittent naval bombardments of city and its defences by the US fleet

Palma Soriano

San Luis — Cubanitas

El Caney

El Cobre

Gascon Creek

Saranilla & Marasa Railway

San Juan River

El Caney

Siboney

Juragua Iron Company Railway

Morro Castle

N

— — — Trench & rifle pit

☐ Blockhouse abandoned

| 0 | 1000 yds |
| 0 | 1000 m |

After the battle of 1 July, Shafter was unsure whether he could hold his positions. With the arrival of Lawton's missing division and at the insistence of Gen. Wheeler, he elected to remain on the ridge. Kent's division deployed to the left of the main section of San Juan Heights, and Lawton's division was placed to the north and north-west. The Cavalry Division held the main ridge. After the Spanish fleet was destroyed on 3 July, a Spanish column fought its way through from the west to reinforce the defenders. The Cuban insurgents deployed in that sector had failed to prevent the column reaching the city. Shafter therefore ordered Ludlow's brigade into a position where it would seal the escape route. Trapped and cut off from their water supply, the Spanish were forced to choose between starvation and capitulation. After a series of temporary armistices and naval bombardments, the Spanish agreed to discuss surrender terms on 12 July.

cruiser, USS _Brooklyn_, and then in the confusion the remaining Spanish ships could make good their escape to the west.

Mass was held at dawn on 3 July 1898, and at 8:00am the small Spanish fleet weighed anchor. Observers on the shore noted that one battleship and Admiral Sampson's flagship were no longer on blockade but were several miles to the west. This would increase the Spanish chances of escape, but the odds were still suicidal. At 8:45am, the flagship hoisted the signals 'Sortie in the prescribed order' and 'Viva España!' and led the way towards the harbour entrance. As they got underway the Admiral's aide was heard to exclaim: 'Pobre España!' (Poor Spain!)

At 9:35am, American lookouts spotted the ships emerging in line from the harbour, and alarm bells rang throughout the fleet. Admiral Sampson in the cruiser USS _New York_ was about five miles to the east when the Spanish fleet sortied, so Rear-Admiral Schley was the officer in charge. Confirming that Sampson was nowhere in sight, Schley in the USS _Brooklyn_ gave the order to open fire, and to steam towards the enemy, with the words 'Go right for them!'.

The Spanish speeded up as they emerged from the harbour at six-minute intervals and turned to starboard. The destroyers headed eastward at full speed, while the _Infanta Maria Teresa_ headed straight for Schley's flagship. The USS _Brooklyn_ realised she was the target of a possible ramming, and when the two flagships were a minute's steaming apart, the American cruiser turned hard starboard to avoid the Spanish ship. All the other American warships were turning to port to pursue the Spanish, and the _Brooklyn_ turned right into the path of the battleship USS _Texas_. The battleship's captain ordered full astern and narrowly avoided a collision, while the USS _Brooklyn_ completed turning in a circle.

By 10:10am, both squadrons were sailing on roughly parallel courses 2,500 yards apart, with the Spanish slightly ahead of most of the American ships. Sampson in the USS _New York_ was steaming full ahead to join the battle. Salvoes crashed around both fleets, but the heavier

American guns scored crucial hits. A 13 in. shell from the USS *Iowa* quickly knocked out the rear turret of the *Infanta Maria Teresa*. In return, shells from the *Cristobal Colon* hit the USS *Iowa* twice, forcing her to reduce speed. By now the concentrated fire of several American warships was raking the Spanish flagship. The Spanish gamble had failed.

By 10:15am, the *Infanta Maria Teresa* was blazing from stem to stern. Her magazines flooded, she turned and ran for the beach, and hauled down her colours. The battle had been raging for less than

THE SORTIE OF THE
SPANISH FLEET AT THE BATTLE
OF SANTIAGO
Shortly after 9:30am on the morning of 3 July 1898, lookouts on ships of the American fleet saw their Spanish adversaries emerge from the entrance to Santiago Harbour. The lead ship was the Spanish flagship *Infanta Maria Teresa* which tried to ram the fastest American ship, USS *Brooklyn*.

INSET **The naval battle of Santiago, as drawn by a war artist on board the USS *Indiana*. The Spanish ships are to the right of the picture. Drawing by Carlton T. Chapman from *Harper's Weekly*, July 1898. (Monroe County Public Library)**

DAVID RICKMAN

As the other American ships steamed to close with the enemy, the USS *Brooklyn* turned away in a circle, narrowly avoiding a collision with an American battleship. Both sides started firing, although many of the Spanish shells were defective. As 13 in. shells from the American battleships crashed repeatedly into the Spanish cruisers who were trying to flee at full speed, the action closed to a range of less than a mile. Slugging it out at point-blank range, the Spanish ships got the worst of the exchange, and fire was concentrated on each ship in turn, reducing them to burning hulks. Within an hour of the start of the battle, two Spanish cruisers were aground and burning. The rest of the Spanish squadron would be destroyed within the next hour, with the exception of the cruiser *Cristobal Colon*. The last of the four cruisers to sortie, she avoided heavy damage and continued her escape to the west. By 1:30pm the pursuing American warships overhauled her, and she too was destroyed.

an hour. The *Almirante Oquendo* was next to go. The rearmost of the four Spanish cruisers, she was fired on repeatedly by three American battleships. As fires threatened to ignite her magazine, she too was run aground onto the beach to the west of the flagship, and surrendered. Only two cruisers now remained.

The Spanish destroyers *Furor* and *Pluton* were essentially ignored by the larger cruisers, but had been hit by fire from passing ships. The armed yacht *Gloucester* finished them off, the *Pluton* running aground and the *Furor* sinking in deep water shortly after 11.00am.

The USS *Brooklyn* closed within 1,000 yards of the slower *Vizcaya*, and the two slugged it out until a shell detonated the Spanish ship's bow torpedo tubes: at 11:05am she ran for the beach, racked by fires and secondary explosions. Cheers from the crew of the *Texas* were cut short by her captain, who yelled: 'Don't cheer, boys! Those poor devils are dying.' The USS *Brooklyn* and USS *Oregon* set off after the remaining *Cristobal Colon*, and after a two-hour chase to the west, she too was forced to beach herself.

The Spanish squadron had been completely annihilated. As the guns fell silent, launches were sent to rescue the Spanish sailors from the sharks, and the Cuban insurgents lining the shore. The gallant Admiral Cervera himself was rescued and taken aboard the USS *Iowa* where the victors cheered their former adversary. Of the 2,227 Spanish sailors who sailed that morning, 323 had died and the remainder had been either wounded or taken prisoner. Only one American sailor was killed. The victory was complete.

THE SIEGE OF SANTIAGO

Following the capture of San Juan Heights, the Americans invested Santiago, throwing up fresh entrenchments along the Heights, bringing up Lawton's Division and placing Garçia's Cubans to the west of the city. A request to surrender the city was rejected, and after three days of skirmishing, both sides settled down to a siege. Apart from 10,000 Spaniards in the city, another 20,000 were scattered throughout the province, and Shafter was worried they might suddenly appear in his rear, between him and the beachhead.

Although they never materialised, on 3 July a relief column led by Col. Escario fought its way through to Santiago from the west, bringing weary troops and meagre supplies. Toral now had to feed 13,500 troops and 25,000 civilians. On 4 July Shafter and Toral negotiated a four-day truce to allow the evacuation of civilians: over 20,000 left the city, to be housed in a makeshift refugee camp which was established at El Caney. As the American army was on half rations, they could do little more than the Spanish for the hapless civilians. Shafter requested more men and supplies, and his sick list grew daily.

Although life was bad for the Americans, it was unbearable for the Santiago defenders. With their water supply cut off, no food and precious little ammunition, the Spanish position was untenable. Although they held good defensive positions and could resist any American assault, morale was crumbling. On 8 July Toral proposed to surrender if his troops could march away to a nearby town. Although Shafter wanted to accept, the politicians in Washington refused. The siege continued, and naval bombardments caused civilian casualties but few military losses. Shafter offered another truce on 11 July, and proposed to ship the Spanish back to Spain instead of allowing them to walk away. The Spaniards wanted to save face and, with fever casualties mounting, Shafter, now joined by Gen. Miles, wanted a quick resolution of the campaign. After further negotiations between the two generals and Washington and Havana, Toral accepted Shafter's terms. The Spanish would capitulate: the term 'surrender' was to be avoided.

On 13 July the staff officers of both armies met under a large tree between the lines to discuss terms. After a further flurry of international telegrams, on 17 July the Spanish marched out of the city and into

The wreck of the Spanish cruiser *Vizcaya* on the day after the Battle of Santiago. The fearful damage is evident, as is the effect of the explosion which ripped out her aft turret. (National Archives)

captivity. The Spanish surrender came too late to prevent the spread of yellow fever, and by the end of the month over 4,000 soldiers were in hospital. If the Spanish had been able to hold on for another few weeks they might have realised their plan of watching the American army waste away from disease. Roosevelt led the fight in the press corps to have the force recalled, and the War Department capitulated. The troops were recalled, and on 7 August the first ships set sail for home. Reinforcements of 'Negro' troops and National Guardsmen from the Deep South were left to garrison Santiago and guard the prisoners, as these troops were apparently less susceptible to fever than the others.

The conclusion of the campaign did not directly bring about the end of the war. 140,000 Spanish troops still remained in Cuba. Gen. Miles launched a virtually bloodless invasion of Puerto Rico during July and August of 1898. The blockade of Cuba continued and plans were redrawn for an assault on Havana. In the Philippines, Manila was captured, and the Pacific islands of Guam and Saipan surrendered without a fight. The Spanish public was increasingly opposed to the continuation of the blood-letting, and on 12 August an armistice was signed. Peace talks continued throughout the year, until the final peace treaty was signed on 10 December 1898. The terms were that the United States would annexe the Philippines, the Pacific Islands and Puerto Rico in return for a compensation fee of $20 million. It would continue to occupy Cuba until independence was granted, and the Spanish army would be repatriated. Despite criticism of imperialism, the US Senate approved the terms. The United States was now a global power.

For Spain, the outcome was an unmitigated disaster. Apart from the loss of prestige, territory and lives, the war had another long-term impact. The army felt let down by the people and politicians, and as a result it became more politicised. This, combined with industrial growth and political instability, helped sow the seeds for the Spanish Civil War (1936–39).

The Americans basked in their new position as a world power, and Hawaii and Panama were soon added to the list of overseas territories. The Spanish American War set a precedent for involvement in the Caribbean and the Pacific and set the American battle lines for war in the Pacific between 1941–5. American involvement in the Caribbean still continues today.

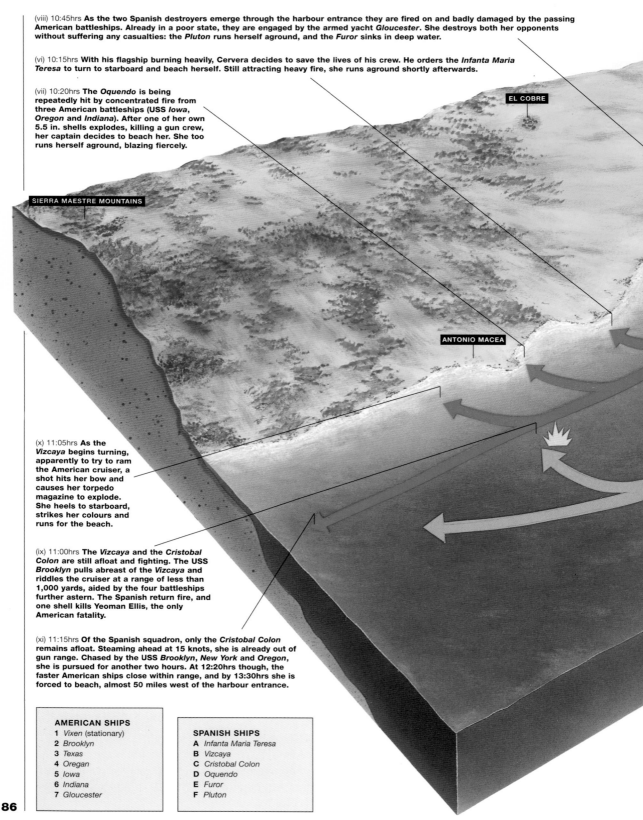

(viii) 10:45hrs **As the two Spanish destroyers emerge through the harbour entrance they are fired on and badly damaged by the passing American battleships. Already in a poor state, they are engaged by the armed yacht** *Gloucester*. **She destroys both her opponents without suffering any casualties: the** *Pluton* **runs herself aground, and the** *Furor* **sinks in deep water.**

(vi) 10:15hrs **With his flagship burning heavily, Cervera decides to save the lives of his crew. He orders the** *Infanta Maria Teresa* **to turn to starboard and beach herself. Still attracting heavy fire, she runs aground shortly afterwards.**

(vii) 10:20hrs **The** *Oquendo* **is being repeatedly hit by concentrated fire from three American battleships (USS** *Iowa*, *Oregon* **and** *Indiana*). **After one of her own 5.5 in. shells explodes, killing a gun crew, her captain decides to beach her. She too runs herself aground, blazing fiercely.**

EL COBRE

SIERRA MAESTRE MOUNTAINS

ANTONIO MACEA

(x) 11:05hrs **As the** *Vizcaya* **begins turning, apparently to try to ram the American cruiser, a shot hits her bow and causes her torpedo magazine to explode. She heels to starboard, strikes her colours and runs for the beach.**

(ix) 11:00hrs **The** *Vizcaya* **and the** *Cristobal Colon* **are still afloat and fighting. The USS** *Brooklyn* **pulls abreast of the** *Vizcaya* **and riddles the cruiser at a range of less than 1,000 yards, aided by the four battleships further astern. The Spanish return fire, and one shell kills Yeoman Ellis, the only American fatality.**

(xi) 11:15hrs **Of the Spanish squadron, only the** *Cristobal Colon* **remains afloat. Steaming ahead at 15 knots, she is already out of gun range. Chased by the USS** *Brooklyn*, *New York* **and** *Oregon*, **she is pursued for another two hours. At 12:20hrs though, the faster American ships close within range, and by 13:30hrs she is forced to beach, almost 50 miles west of the harbour entrance.**

AMERICAN SHIPS	SPANISH SHIPS
1 *Vixen* (stationary)	**A** *Infanta Maria Teresa*
2 *Brooklyn*	**B** *Vizcaya*
3 *Texas*	**C** *Cristobal Colon*
4 *Oregan*	**D** *Oquendo*
5 *Iowa*	**E** *Furor*
6 *Indiana*	**F** *Pluton*
7 *Gloucester*	

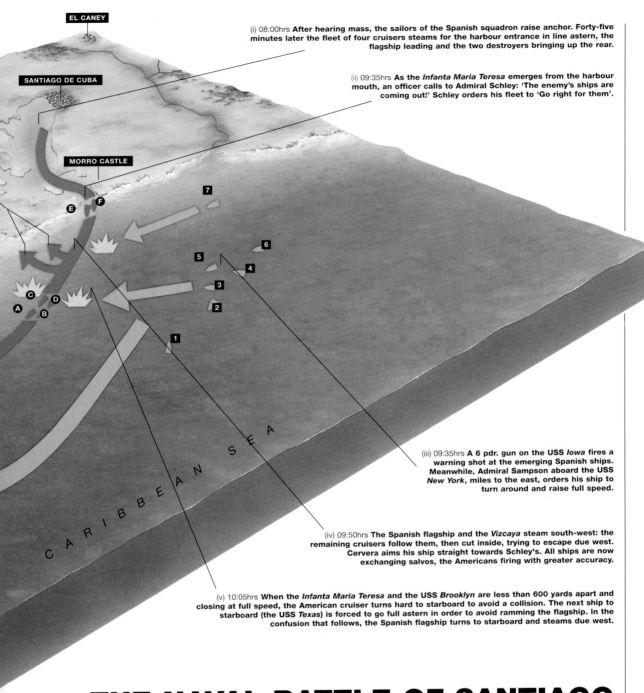

EL CANEY

SANTIAGO DE CUBA

MORRO CASTLE

(i) 08:00hrs **After hearing mass, the sailors of the Spanish squadron raise anchor. Forty-five minutes later the fleet of four cruisers steams for the harbour entrance in line astern, the flagship leading and the two destroyers bringing up the rear.**

(ii) 09:35hrs **As the *Infanta Maria Teresa* emerges from the harbour mouth, an officer calls to Admiral Schley: 'The enemy's ships are coming out!' Schley orders his fleet to 'Go right for them'.**

(iii) 09:35hrs **A 6 pdr. gun on the USS *Iowa* fires a warning shot at the emerging Spanish ships. Meanwhile, Admiral Sampson aboard the USS *New York*, miles to the east, orders his ship to turn around and raise full speed.**

(iv) 09:50hrs **The Spanish flagship and the *Vizcaya* steam south-west: the remaining cruisers follow them, then cut inside, trying to escape due west. Cervera aims his ship straight towards Schley's. All ships are now exchanging salvos, the Americans firing with greater accuracy.**

(v) 10:05hrs **When the *Infanta Maria Teresa* and the USS *Brooklyn* are less than 600 yards apart and closing at full speed, the American cruiser turns hard to starboard to avoid a collision. The next ship to starboard (the USS *Texas*) is forced to go full astern in order to avoid ramming the flagship. In the confusion that follows, the Spanish flagship turns to starboard and steams due west.**

CARIBBEAN SEA

N

THE NAVAL BATTLE OF SANTIAGO
3 July 1898 08:00–11:15hrs

The capture of San Juan Heights made the position of the Spanish naval squadron untenable. Forced with the option of being sunk at anchor by American artillery, or breaking through the US naval blockade, Admiral Cervera reluctantly decided to sortie. The resulting naval action was short, brutal and one-sided. Within hours the American fleet had inflicted a crushing defeat on the Spaniards, who fought their unequal battle with notable courage.

CHRONOLOGY

1898

25 January	USS *Maine* sent from Key West to Havana to help protect American citizens
15 February	USS *Maine* blows up in Havana harbour: 266 die
9 March	Senate approves a 'War Fund' of $50 million
25 March	President McKinley announces USS *Maine* blown up by a mine
19 April	Congress supports a call for Cuban independence, and the use of US force to help achieve it
21 April	US navy leaves Key West to commence blockade of Cuba
23 April	Spain declares war on the United States; President McKinley calls for 125,000 volunteers
25 April	United States formally declares war on Spain
1 May	Commodore Dewey destroys Spanish Asiatic Fleet at Manila Bay
12 June	Gen. Shafter's V Corps embark at Tampa, bound for Santiago
22 June	US V Corps lands at Daiquiri
23 June	Siboney occupied and forward supply base established
24 June	Skirmish at Las Guasimas
26 June	Americans occupy Sevilla
27 June	Gen. Shafter lands and establishes headquarters at Sevilla
30 June	Army moves forward to El Pozo and Marianage
1 July	Battles of El Caney and San Juan Hill
4:00am	Kent and Sumner's divisions march towards San Juan Heights
6:35am	Capron's battery opens fire on El Caney

American troops in the trenches lining San Juan Heights. The blockhouse is in the background, and Santiago is off to the right. The shallow trenches indicate that the photograph was taken within days of the capture of the Heights. (National Archives)

8:20am	Grimes's battery opens fire on San Juan blockhouse
8:25am	Spanish on San Juan Heights fire on Grimes's battery position
9:00am	Major firefight ensues around El Caney
9:15am	Spanish start firing on main US column on Camino Real
10:50am	US column reaches Bloody Ford. Troops deploy along riverbank
11:00am	Lull in fighting at El Caney
Noon	Gen. Shafter orders Gen. Lawton to rejoin main force
12:15pm	Waiting US troops along San Juan River take heavy casualties
1:00pm	Firing begins again at El Caney: assault on San Juan Hill ordered
1:05pm	Roosevelt and assorted cavalrymen launch attack on Kettle Hill
1:10pm	Main assault on San Juan Hill – immediately pinned down
1:15pm	Kettle Hill captured: Gatling gun battery opens up on San Juan Hill
1:20pm	Fresh assault on San Juan Hill launched
1:30pm	San Juan blockhouse in US hands: assault on El Viso Fort is launched
1:35pm	Roosevelt's fresh assault on northern section of the Heights
1:45pm	El Viso captured: San Juan Heights in US hands
2:00pm	Spanish withdraw to final defence line at El Caney: US troops on San Juan Heights subjected to heavy Spanish fire
3:00pm	Final Spanish resistance at El Caney is overcome: Kent and Sumner's divisions dig-in along San Juan Heights
3 July	Naval battle of Santiago: Spanish squadron destroyed
17 July	Gen. Toral surrenders all Spanish forces in Santiago Province
25 July	American troops land on Puerto Rico
12 August	Armistice signed and blockade of Cuba lifted
18 October	United States annexes Puerto Rico
2 November	Spain agrees to cede the Philippines to the United States
10 December	Peace treaty signed in Paris

BIBLIOGRAPHY

A number of comprehensive works are available on the Spanish American War, including published first-hand accounts.

Blow, Michael, *A Ship to Remember, The Maine and the Spanish American War* (New York, 1992) Concentrates on the causes of the outbreak of war and the loss of the *Maine*.

Brown, Christopher H., *The Correspondent's War: Journalists in the Spanish-American War* (New York, 1967) An interesting slant on the conflict.

Davis, Richard Harding, *The Cuban and Puerto Rican Campaigns* (New York, 1898) Highly critical but excellent journalist's first-hand account.

Feur, A.B., *The Spanish-American War at Sea* (Connecticut, 1995) Detailed naval account

Teijerio, José Muller y, *The Battle and Capitulation of Santiago de Cuba* (Washington DC, 1898) A rare Spanish account published in English.

Nofi, Albert A., *The Spanish–American War, 1898* (Pennsylvania, 1996) An excellent and concise account, with technical appendices and useful military information.

O'Toole, G.J.A., *The Spanish War: An American Epic* (New York, 1984) A competent general account.

Post, Charles J., *The Little War of Private Post* (New York, 1960) Revealing first-hand account by a soldier in the 71st New York Regiment, published by a descendant.

Roosevelt, Theodore, *The Rough Riders* (several editions) How 'Teddy' won the war single-handed. Famous for attacks on other participants.

Trask, David F., *The War with Spain in 1898* (New York, 1981) Detailed modern history, emphasising diplomatic and political decisions.

THE BATTLEFIELD TODAY

Today, Santiago de Cuba is a large industrial seaport, with factories, docks and warehouses spread around the shore of Santiago Bay. Major housing areas have spread up the slopes of San Juan Heights and the hills north and north-west of the city. Central Santiago remains much as it was in 1898, and the historic quarter is a popular tourist attraction. The site of the blockhouse on San Juan Hill itself now forms the centre of a battlefield park, established in the 1920s. The blockhouse itself is long gone, replaced by a replica of the fortification. American and Spanish artillery pieces dot the park, together with palm trees, statues and plaques. The principal monument is the Tomb of the Unknown Mambi (Insurgent). Another is dedicated to Cuban revolutionaries 'and the generous American soldiers who sealed a covenant of liberty and fraternity'. Visitors can gain a feeling for the topography of the battlefield from views north-east towards El Caney and east towards El Pozo.

The side of the hill facing the city itself now contains an amusement park, a zoo and a hospital. Set amid a residential area, the former Canovar Barracks have been replaced by the Hotel San Juan, formerly the Leningrad Hotel, a resort built for Soviet tourists. This prevents any visitor gaining an impression of the extent of the siege lines, although the tree marking the site of the capitulation talks has been preserved. The main battlefield area where the US army stormed Kettle Hill and the Bloody Ford remains largely intact, although residential and industrial buildings obscure the topography by the riverbank and Kettle Hill. What is surprising is the short distance between the cardinal points of the battlefield, and the steepness of the slope on San Juan Hill.

Further to the south towards Aguadores, the airport occupies the coastal area leading up to the harbour mouth. The Morro Castle still dominates the harbour entrance, and is a popular tourist attraction, although its supporting gun batteries have been replaced by

Wounded Spanish prisoners after the battle of San Juan. These soldiers reflect the ethnic mix of the Spanish army, and served in the Provisional Battalion of Puerto Rico, which garrisoned the blockhouse. (National Archives)

Spanish and American officers discussing the terms of the Spanish capitulation. In the background are Generals Shafter, Wheeler and Toral. The 'Surrender Tree', where the agreement was signed, is off to the right of the photograph. (National Archives)

hotels. The village of El Caney has been swallowed up by development, and apart from the ruins of El Viso, the church and the central plaza, no trace of the battlefield remains. Las Guasimas is not as developed as El Caney, although a sculpture garden dominates the hillside which held the main Spanish positions. The villages of Siboney and Daiquiri are also largely unchanged, although a hotel complex at Daiquiri dominates the hill above the village.

Surprisingly, traces of the naval battle can still be seen. The Spanish cruiser *Vizcaya* still lies beached on the shore to the west of Santiago, and the other wrecks (apart from the Spanish flagship which was towed away) provide an attraction for divers. The historical museum in Santiago contains displays which cover the campaign, although the role played by the Cuban insurgents dominates the narrative. A maritime museum contains relics from the Spanish ships.

In the United States, apart from the hotel in Tampa that served as V Corps headquarters, and traces of 1898-period US navy buildings and fortifications in Key West, no trace of the conflict remains. A handful of museums, including the US Ordnance Museum, the US Naval Museum and the US Signal Corps Museum, contain displays relating to the conflict. Otherwise, the war seems to be long forgotten.

ORDERS OF BATTLE
SANTIAGO CAMPAIGN 1898

THE US ARMY

UNITED STATES V CORPS (Maj.Gen. Shafter)

FIRST DIVISION (Brig.Gen. Kent)

1st Brigade (Brig.Gen. Hawkins)
6th US Infantry Regt. (464 men)
16th US Infantry Regt. (630 men)
71st New York Volunteer Regt. (958 men)

2nd Brigade (Col. Pearson)
2nd US Infantry Regt. (619 men)
10th US Infantry Regt. (471 men)
21st US Infantry Regt. (467 men)

3rd Brigade (Col. Wikoff)
9th US Infantry Regt. (487 men)
13th US Infantry Regt. (460 men)
24th US Infantry Regt. (534 men)

SECOND DIVISION (Maj.Gen. Lawton)

1st Brigade (Brig.Gen. Ludlow)
8th US Infantry Regt. (460 men)
22nd US Infantry Regt. (460 men)
2nd Massachusetts Volunteer Infantry Regt. (460 men)

2nd Brigade (Col. Miles)
1st US Infantry Regt. (460 men)
4th US Infantry Regt. (460 men)
25th US Infantry Regt. (460 men)

3rd Brigade (Brig.Gen. Chaffee)
7th US Infantry Regt. (460 men)
12th US Infantry Regt. (460 men)
17th US Infantry Regt. (460 men)

Independent Brigade (Brig.Gen. Bates)
Attached to Second Division
3rd US Infantry Regt. (460 men)
20th US Infantry Regt. (460 men)

CAVALRY DIVISION (Maj.Gen. Wheeler)
Sumner took over for battle

1st Brigade (Brig.Gen. Young) Wood replaced Young for battle
1st US Cavalry Regt. (522 men)
10th US Cavalry Regt. (472 men)
1st US Volunteer Cavalry Regt. (542 men)

2nd Brigade (Brig.Gen. Sumner)
Col. Carroll took over for the battle
3rd US Cavalry Regt. (442 men)
6th US Cavalry Regt. (443 men)
9th US Cavalry Regt. (219 men)

ATTACHED ARTILLERY (Corps Assets)

Grimes's Bty. (4 x 3.2 in. guns)
Best's Bty. (4 x 3.2 in. guns)
Capron's Bty. (4 x 3.2 in. guns)
Parkhurst's Bty. (4 x 3.2 in. guns)
Parker's Bty. (4 x Gatling guns)

OTHER CORPS ASSETS:

HQ Staff (17 men)
1st Sqn. 2nd US Cavalry (mounted) (265 men)
Engineer Bn. (C & E Companies) (200 men)
Signal Detachment (including Balloon) (90 men)
Hospital Corps (275 men)

BEACHHEAD GARRISON, SIBONEY (Brig.Gen. Henry M. Duffield)

9th Massachusetts Volunteer Regt. (840 men)
8th Ohio Volunteer Regt. (c.1100 men)
33rd Michigan Volunteer Regt. (c.1000 men)
34th Michigan Volunteer Regt. (c.640 men)
E Bty. US 1st Artillery (4-8 in. Mortars)

Raising the American flag over the Reina Mercedes Barracks in Santiago de Cuba. Leaving Leonard Wood in charge, Shafter would take his army home within days of the capitulation. (National Archives)

THE SPANISH ARMY

SPANISH ARMY UNITS
Santiago District (Gen. Linares)
Gen. Toral after 1 July

SANTIAGO AND ENVIRONS

1st Provisional Bn. of Puerto Rico (c.600 men)

4th Bn. Talavera Peninsular Regt. (c.600 men)

1st Bn. San Fernando Regt. (No. 11) (c.750 men)

1st Bn. Asia Regt. (No. 55) (c.1,000 men)

1st Bn. Constituçional Regt. (No. 29) (c.300 men) Detachment

1st and 2nd Bns. Cuba Regt. (No. 65) (c.2,000 men)

1st Bn. Simancas Regt. (No. 64) (c.125 men) Detachment

Guerrilla Companies, Tercios 1 & 2 (c.2,650 men) 50% mounted

1st Cavalry Regt. (mounted) (c.250 men)

6th Bty. 10th Fortress Artillery Bn.

(c.300 men in Coastal Batteries)

6th Bty. 4th Horse Artillery Regt. (4 x 75mm guns) two at San Juan, two at El Caney

1st Bty. 5th Foot Artillery Regt. (4 x 90mm guns)

Naval Brigade (from squadron) (c.1,000 men)

Engineers (c.550 men)

Staff (c.110 men)

Medical Corps (c.130 men)

Guardia Civil (c.200 men)

EL CANEY GARRISON
(Gen. Vara del Rey)

3 Companies, 1st Bn., Constituçional Regt. (29th) (360 men)

1 Company, Cuban Loyalist Irregulars (70 men) mounted

Detachment, 1st Bn., Simancas Regt. (No. 64) (40 men)

Detachment, 1st Cavalry Regt. (50 men) mounted

Section, 4th Artillery Bn. (2 x 75mm Placencia guns)

INDEX

Figures in **bold** refer to illustrations